I0032250

PUBLICATIONS OF THE
BUREAU OF BUSINESS AND ECONOMIC RESEARCH

Previously published in this series:

application of
linear programming
to the theory of the firm

APPLICATION OF LINEAR PROGRAMMING TO THE THEORY OF THE FIRM

INCLUDING AN ANALYSIS OF MONOPOLISTIC FIRMS BY NON-LINEAR PROGRAMMING

ROBERT DORFMAN

A PUBLICATION OF THE BUREAU OF BUSINESS AND ECONOMIC RESEARCH, UNIVERSITY OF CALIFORNIA

PUBLISHED BY THE UNIVERSITY OF CALIFORNIA PRESS
BERKELEY AND LOS ANGELES   NINETEEN FIFTY ONE

University of California Press
Berkeley and Los Angeles, California
Cambridge University Press, London, England

Copyright 1951
By the Regents of the University of California

BUREAU OF BUSINESS AND ECONOMIC RESEARCH

William Crum, Chairman

Robert A. Brady   Charles A. Gulick   Roy W. Jastram   Maurice Moonitz

Sanford A. Mosk, Acting Director

The opinions expressed in this study
are those of the author. The functions of the
Bureau of Business and Economic Research
are confined to facilitating the prosecution of
independent scholarly research by members of the faculty.

This monograph, except for the last part of chapter iii, was pre-
pared as a doctoral dissertation in the Department of Economics,
University of California. The committee in charge of the research was headed successively by Professors William Fellner and
R. A. Gordon. Chapter iv, especially, bears the imprint of Professor Gordon's strict and constructive criticisms. Another member of the committee, Professor G. C. Evans of the Department of
Mathematics, served as the guardian of the author's mathematical
conscience. Whatever mathematical elegance the treatment contains must be credited to the high standards which Professor
Evans imposed and insisted on.

All work in the field of linear programming must be deeply
indebted to Dr. George B. Dantzig of the Department of the Air
Force, who opened up the field and has been one of its most productive investigators. But Dr. Dantzig's contribution to the
present monograph goes far beyond that. He gave much of his
time to instructing the author in the concepts and methods of
linear programming and after the research was under way allowed
his patience to be imposed on many times when difficulties beyond the mathematical competence of the author threatened to
bring the project to an ignominious halt. Professor A. W.
Tucker, Princeton University, and Professor E. W. Barankin,
University of California, were also consulted about mathematical
difficulties, and the author is gratified to note that each of
them subsequently undertook mathematical studies of first importance in problems suggested by this thesis. Professor
Tucker, especially, by his pioneering study of "Non-Linear Programming," cleared the way for the treatment of quadratic programming, which appears in chapter iii.

If this volume were dedicated to anyone, it would be to the
officers and officials who staff the headquarters of the United
States Air Force. These far-sighted men, faced with the difficulties of administering one of the largest integrated organizations
in the world, have had the vision required to turn away from traditional methods of administration and to encourage an ambitious

program of research into the theory of programming. The research whose results are reported in this monograph was originally undertaken as part of that research program and was inspired to a great extent by the needs of the Air Force. It is the author's earnest wish that these results may assist in some small measure in easing and improving the work of Air Force headquarters. But, of course, the author also feels that the theories here developed invite far wider application.

I wish to thank the various publishers who have given permission for the use of quotations from their publications, including:

Harper & Brothers for permission to quote from Kenneth E. Boulding, *Economic Analysis,* 1941.

Harvard University Press for permission to quote from Paul A. Samuelson, *Foundations of Economic Analysis,* 1948.

Houghton Mifflin Company for permission to quote from Frank H. Knight, *Risk, Uncertainty and Profit,* 1921.

The Macmillan Company for permission to quote from Joan Robinson, *The Economics of Imperfect Competition,* 1948.

Oxford University Press, Inc., for permission to quote from J. R. Hicks, *Value and Capital,* 1941.

University of California   R. D.
Berkeley, California
April 13, 1951

Contents

- - - - - - - - - - - - - - - - - - - -

CHAPTER I

Two Approaches
to the Theory of the Firm

1. *Historical Perspective.*

The modern theory of the firm as expounded by Chamberlin (3)*, Hicks (16), Robinson (31), Samuelson (32), Viner (38), *et al.*, traces its lineage back to Ricardo's discussion of the problems of English agriculture a century and a half ago. Ricardo and his contemporary, Malthus, share credit for the development of the concept of " deceasing returns," the progenitor of the modern U-shaped cost curve. The classicists also used the idea of incremental variation of factors of production and thus set the stage for the modern " marginal" analysis. The fact that an analytic apparatus which was inspired by the predicament of early nineteenth-century English agriculture is so deeply embedded in the analysis of modern industrial problems calls for a reconsideration of the appropriateness of the model.

Ricardo's theory (30) was based on a highly abstracted model of a single type of farming: English wheat cultivation. He grouped all things necessary for the cultivation of wheat into three factors of production: land, labor, and capital. He assumed that these factors of production could be combined in, essentially, any proportions desired. The technical process involved was considered from a broad point of view which ignored the existence of subsidiary steps and intermediate products; the three necessary factors were applied and after a proper interval the final product emerged. The entire process resulted in a single, homogeneous commodity—wheat.

---

*Numbers in parentheses refer to the references at the end of the volume.

Ricardo applied this model, essentially, to calculate the distribution of product between the landowner, who supplied the land, and the farmer, who provided the capital. He assumed that the total quantity of land was fixed and this total could be subdivided into the amounts of land of first, second, third, etc., qualities, which were also fixed. It is now that the technique of incremental variation and the postulate of decreasing returns enter. As new capital seeks to enter agricultural production, it may be applied to new, and less productive, land or to the more intensive cultivation of land already in use. In either case, it will give rise to a smaller physical product per unit than capital previously applied. An increased application of capital to a fixed supply of land will therefore tend to raise rents, lower interest, and increase the real cost of production. It is not necessary for our purposes to describe Ricardo's theory further; the foregoing is sufficient to show that it contained the essentials of the modern analysis of the valuation of factors of production and the allocation of resources.

This model answered rather well to the problem which interested Ricardo. Almost as soon as it was laid down, however, economists began to apply it to a broader range of questions and to make the necessary emendations. All that was necessary, really, was to combine the Ricardian technique of analysis with Say's concept of firm (34) which purchased the services of the three factors of production in a competitive market. Within a generation Nassau Senior adapted the Ricardian mode of analysis to the study of industrial production by treating the three factors of production more symmetrically than Ricardo had (35). Contemporaneously with Senior, Cournot made the pioneer application of the differential calculus to the theory of the firm (5), but this did not bear fruit until the 1870's when Jevons (17), Menger (27), and their followers introduced the formal methods of marginal analysis. As applied to the theory of production, the marginal analysis was an improvement more in form than in content, however. The marginalist contribution was essentially a more symmetrical, compact, and formal technique for handling the received Ricardian model. The marginalist analysis of the behavior of the firm and the allocation of productive resources has enjoyed practically complete acceptance for the past seventy-five years, so that it is fair to say that in spite of more than a century of refinement, the analysis of production to this very day is based upon the original Ricardian-Malthusian concepts.

The classical Ricardian analysis was a study of long-run economic equilibrium, of " the high theme of economic progress. " But, as our quick survey has just indicated, as it passed through successive hands it evolved into a theory of entrepreneurial behavior, that is into an explanation of the factors which govern an entrepreneur's decisions. In the 1930's this application of the theory underwent rapid refinement, especially at the hands of Chamberlin (3), Robinson (31), Viner (38), and their followers. A reaction against this refined application of the marginal approach is now in progress. Hall and Hitch (14) and Lester (25) have made field studies of business decision-making which show that the considerations which businessmen take into account are quite different from the concepts of the marginal analysis and perhaps inconsistent with it. Gordon (13) and Eiteman (11) have reinforced these doubts by showing that it is hardly conceivable that businessmen can obtain the information which the marginal analysis assumes they have at their disposal. Dean (10) and Lester (25) have made empirical studies which raise questions as to the validity of the shape of the short-run production curve assumed by the marginal analysis.

It deserves to be repeated, of course, that this array of criticism of the marginal analysis bears most particularly on its application to entrepreneurial behavior in the relatively short run, but, since all decisions of individuals and firms are short-run decisions, these criticisms concern the entire theory of the firm.

The critics have also attempted the constructive task of answering the question: If the marginal analysis does not explain entrepreneurial behavior, what does? The strong influence of custom and the concept of a "fair profit" have been emphasized by Hall and Hitch and Lester on the basis of their empirical studies. Eiteman has sketched a theory which is based on the concept of maintaining normal inventories and a normal rate of turnover of working capital. A very ambitious attempt was made by von Neumann and Morgenstern (40) to explain entrepreneurial and market behavior in terms of a theory of competitive strategy. Unfortunately, the empirical theories all rest on the contention that businessmen attempt to maintain some sort of "normal" relationships in the price structures of their industries and the financial structures of their

firms. The process by which these norms come to be established
or modified is still largely conjectural. In essence these theories assert that any equilibrium position, once attained, ac-
quires a sort of social inertia which helps to perpetuate it.
It is perhaps this superficial level of explanation, this aban-
donment of the maximization principle in favor of the non-ration-
al following of sociological norms, which has deterred economists
by and large from accepting the conclusions of this school as a
satisfactory explanation of entrepreneurial behavior.

The von Neumann and Morgenstern theory attempts to supplant the
marginal analysis from another direction. It is ultra-rational.
It assumes that all businessmen are oligopolists engaged in an un-
remitting strategic struggle, each to maximize his own profits at
the expense of his competitors and the world at large. Unfortunately for this theory, as von Neumann and Morgenstern themselves
show, the rational conclusion of such a struggle is the formation
of monopolistic cartels; the assumption of oligopoly is itself inconsistent with the assumption of complete rationality. Von
Neumann and Morgenstern attempt to salvage the theory by introduc-
ing an irrational element, the so-called "standards of behavior"
(40, p. 40) but these remain ill-defined and do not lead to stable
responses to market situations. Von Neumann and Morgenstern's
theory is open to other criticisms, too, but this is not the
place to review their monumental work.

In recent years interest has been growing in a rather different
approach to economic and managerial problems, the "input-output"
or "linear programming" approach. Even at this writing the content and methodology of linear programming are in so formative a
state that it would be premature to attempt to delimit them. It
represents a confluence of several diverse streams of development:
mathematical studies of the geometry of higher spaces dating back,
probably to Laplace and certainly to Weyl (42), a simple dynamic
economic model due to von Neumann (39), Leontief's matrix description of the interrelations of American industry (23), and Wood and
Dantzig's research into the managerial problems of the Air Force
(9, 36, 37, 43, 44, 45). Research into the theory of games by von
Neumann and others certainly helped pave the way for linear programming which mathematically, though not conceptually, is a closely related problem. In spite of the long existence of these varied
anticipatory developments, the first integration of them into the
viewpoint and the tool which is now called linear programming was
probably achieved by Dantzig in 1947.

The original appearance of linear programming, then, was in the field of scientific management rather than in that of economics (and this may account for the fact that linear programming largely neglects the demand side of economic problems). The interest of economists in the new technique awakened quickly, however, and Koopmans (20 and 22) took the lead in studying the application of linear programming to problems of economic welfare. The present essay appears to be the first attempt to apply linear programming to the short-run behavior of the individual firm or entrepreneur and to assess its value for dealing with this problem.

Linear programming will be described in this book in terms of its relationship to the theory of the firm. The best starting point will be an outline of the formal structure of the marginalist approach to this same theory.

2. *The Marginal Analysis*

The marginal analysis (like linear programming) is concerned with the decisions of an economic unit called a firm. This firm, it is assumed, has just one motive: to maximize its profits, or the excess of its revenues over its expenses. The decisions which the firm has to make are of three sorts: technical decisions, which determine the methods of production to be employed, quantity decisions, which concern the amount of goods to be offered and sold, and marketing decisions which deal with procedures for altering, if possible, the demand curves of the firm's customers. It should be noted that a firm in pure competition cannot affect the prices at which it buys and sells, while a monopolist can determine either the prices at which he buys and sells or the quantities which he buys and sells but not both.

The marketing decisions will not be discussed further in this paper. With the exception of Chamberlin (3, chapter vii), there has been little effort to integrate them with the body of economic doctrine, presumably because the central issues of economics concern the response to the want-pattern of society rather than manipulation of it.

Technical decisions are usually banned from the economic field of discourse and relegated to that of engineering by the assumption that there is some most efficient way to combine given quantities of raw materials to produce a desired bill of products, and that this is the technical procedure which will be adopted. The solution to the technical problems of the firm is regarded as summarized by a "production function." Samuelson presents a typical formulation:

> We assume as given by technical considerations the maximum amount of output, x, which can be produced from any given set of inputs $(v_1, \ldots, v_n)$. This catalogue of possibilities is the production function and may be written
>
> $$x = f(v_1, \ldots, v_n).$$
>
> In general, there will be a maximum output for each set of inputs, and so this function is single-valued, and will be assumed initially to have continuous partial derivatives of desired order. (32, pp. 57, 58).

The formal essence of the marginal analysis of the firm can now be stated very briefly and in somewhat more general terms than Samuelson's. We begin with the firm, which is assumed to be a rational, independent, decision-making unit whose whole objective is to maximize profits. Its field of decision making and the measure of merit of any decisions are defined in terms of production and price functions. Assume that the firm produces m salable commodities by consuming n inputs. Let x_i denote the quantity produced of the ith salable commodity and v_j the quantity consumed of the jth input. We assume also that these quantities are connected by the production or transformation function

0.1 $$f(x_1, \ldots, x_m; v_1, \ldots, v_n) = 0$$

A little care is needed in the definition of this function. For any given set of inputs, $v_1, \ldots, v_n$, there will generally be several technically possible sets of outputs, $x_1, \ldots, x_m$. Assign arbitrary values to $m-1$ of these outputs and determine the largest value of the remaining output which is consistent with equation 0.1. In this manner we are assured that the transformation function will be single-valued, that is, if all the inputs and all but one of the outputs are assigned, then the remaining output is fully determined. It is assumed also that the transformation function is defined over the domain of non-negative inputs and outputs and that within the domain of definition it has continuous partial derivatives of first and second order.

We assume that a price function is associated with each salable commodity and that its value is dependent on the quantities produced of all salable commodities. We denote these functions by:

0.2
$$P_i = P_i (x_1, \ldots, x_m).$$

Then we define gross revenue to be:

0.3
$$r = \sum_{i=1}^{m} P_i x_i.$$

It is assumed that a price function is associated also with each input, and that these functions may be written

0.4
$$q_j = q_j (v_1, \ldots, v_n).$$

The cost of production is then defined to be:

0.5
$$c = \sum_{j=1}^{n} q_j v_j.$$

And finally, profit is defined to be:

0.6
$$\pi = r-c$$

By virtue of the equations 0.1 to 0.6, the profit and all subsidiary variables are seen to be functions of the inputs, v_j and the outputs, x_i. The field of decision is then that region in which all of the v_j and x_i are positive and the objective of the firm is to find that set of v_j and x_i for which π is as great as possible. That is, it is required to find a stationary value of equation 0.6 subject to the restriction of equation 0.1 and to conditions on the second derivatives which will guarantee that the stationary value is a maximum rather than a minimum or a point of inflection. The problem is solved by a straightforward application of Langrange's method. Form the function:

0.7
$$u = r - c - kf(x_1, \ldots, x_m; v_1, \ldots, v_n)$$

and calculate the partial derivatives with respect to each of the inputs and outputs. Let:

$$MR(i) = \frac{dr}{dx_i} = P_i + \sum_{\alpha=1}^{m} x_d \frac{dp_\alpha}{dx_i}$$

denote the marginal revenue obtained by producing an additional unit of the ith output, all other outputs and inputs remaining the same, and

$$MC(j) = \frac{dr}{dv_j} = q_j + \sum_{\beta=1}^{n} v_\beta \frac{dq_\beta}{dv_j}$$

denote the marginal cost of procuring one more unit of the jth input, all other variables remaining the same. Then, taking the partial derivatives of equation 0.7 and equating them to zero, we obtain:

$$MR(i) - k\frac{df}{dx_i} = 0, \qquad i = 1, \ldots, m;$$

$$-MC(j) - k\frac{df}{dv_j} = 0, \qquad j = 1, \ldots, n.$$

The simultaneous solution of these two sets of equations together with equation 0.1 determines the optimum values of all the inputs and all the outputs.

The leading results of this analysis are obtained immediately by finding ratios of pairs of these equations. In this manner we find:

$$0.8 \qquad \frac{MR(i_1)}{MR(i_2)} = -\frac{dx_{i_2}}{dx_{i_1}}$$

which indicates that when the optimum quantities of commodities i_1 and i_2 are being produced, the ratio of their marginal revenues must be equal to the rate of physical substitutability in production of the two commodities.

Similarly, we find for the inputs:

$$0.9 \qquad \frac{MC(j_1)}{MC(j_2)} = -\frac{dv_{j_2}}{dv_{j_1}}$$

which indicates that when optimum quantities of inputs j_1 and j_2 are being consumed, the ratio of their marginal costs must be equal to their physical substitutability in the production function. And, finally, we obtain:

0.10
$$\frac{MC(j)}{MR(i)} = \frac{dx_i}{dv_j}$$

which shows that at the optimum the ratio of the marginal cost of
the jth input to the marginal revenue of the ith output is
equal to the marginal physical productivity of the jth input for
producing the ith output. From this last ratio it follows that:

0.11
$$\frac{1}{MR(i)} = \frac{\dfrac{dx_i}{dv_j}}{MC(j)}$$

which signifies that the number of units of the ith output which
can be obtained by increasing the cost by \$1 is the same, no mat-
ter which input that \$1 is expended on. Further, equation 0.11
shows that \$1 spent on any input will produce a sufficient in-
crease in physical output so that revenue is increased by \$1.

We have now obtained the "first-order" conditions for an optimum production plan. But an analysis based on first derivatives alone cannot guarantee the attainment of a maximum; a local minimum or a stationary value will also satisfy these conditions on the first derivatives. For a local maximum to exist,
the well-known conditions on the second-order derivatives of
equation 0.7 must be satisfied (see, for example, 16, pp. 319-
320). Analysis of these conditions would lead to a more extended discussion than the purposes of this brief survey of the
formal marginalist theory warrant. Such analyses, for cases
somewhat less general than the one discussed above, have been
carried out by Samuelson (32, pp. 61-63) and Hicks (16, chapter
vi and pp. 319-320). The most compact statement of the complete conditions for an optimal production schedule under pure
competition has been given by Hicks:

If the prices of all products and all factors are given to
the enterprise, the quantities of factors it will employ, and
products it will produce, will be given by the condition that
the surplus is a maximum. This implies that it cannot be increased by any type of variation. We shall thus have the
following conditions of equilibrium . . .

(1) Corresponding to the condition price = marginal cost, we
have three sorts of conditions:

(a) The price-ratio between any two products must equal the marginal rate of substitution between the two products (this is now a technical rate of substitution).

(b) The price-ratio between any two factors must equal their marginal rate of substitution.

(c) The price-ratio between any factor and any product must equal the marginal rate of transformation between the factor and the product (that is to say, the marginal product of the factor in terms of this particular product).

(2) Next there are the stability conditions. For the transformation of a factor into a product we shall have the condition of diminishing marginal rate of transformation or diminishing marginal product. For the substitution of one product for another we shall have a condition of "increasing marginal rate of substitution," that is to say, increasing marginal cost in terms of the other product (marginal opportunity cost). For the substitution of one factor for another, "diminishing marginal rate of substitution." (16, pp 86-87).

This quotation summarizes the results of the marginal analysis of the firm's production problem. The entire analysis depends on being able to differentiate the production, revenue, and cost functions with respect to each input and output independently, a mathematical procedure which has operational significance only when corresponding variations of values are possible in the phenomenal world. Such cases do exist in economics, characterized by production situations in which the field of technical choices includes infinitesimal variations of individual inputs and outputs. The classic Ricardian case, agriculture, is an example of such a technological situation. There it is technically feasible to vary the quantities of seed, labor, fertilizer, and the like used per acre over a wide range without altering the method of production in other respects.

But in non-agricultural industries, the case is often otherwise. Machinery, and especially the more advanced types, is likely to be inflexible with regard to the factors which must be combined with it and with regard to the rate and character of its output. Thus, when it has been determined to use a certain number of units of a specific machine, several of the other variables in the production function have been determined at the same time. It will not then be possible to move freely from point to point on the production surface except in an indirect manner. This can be seen as follows. Although any particular industrial process is quite inflexible with regard to the character and quantity of the factors it consumes, there are generally a number of alternative processes, differing in this respect, for attaining the same general result. By combining a number of different processes, a wide variety of factor-input and product-output ratios for the firm as a whole can be attained. For example, in typesetting a linotype machine requires less floorspace per unit of output but more power than a monotype machine. By having some machines of each kind, the space and power facilities of a plant can be utilized fully.

The type of decision which faces a firm using industrial processes is therefore essentially different from the decisions contemplated by the marginal analysis. The firm may decide the extent to which to use each of the types of equipment it owns at any time. In that case any variation in the use of equipment implies simultaneous variation in the use of factors complementary to that equipment. The firm may choose among a number (generally finite) of ways of applying its equipment. Or it may select among a number of types of equipment offered for its purchase. All of these decisions differ in two respects from the kind of decision treated in the marginal analysis. First, they affect the quantities of a group of distinct inputs and outputs simultaneously. Second, the range of choice does not lie along a continuous scale, but involves selection among discrete alternatives. The effects of such decisions are therefore not adequately expressed by the theoretical operation of partial differentiation with respect to the quantities of separate inputs and outputs.

For the study of decisions in such an industrial milieu, an analytic apparatus is required whose structure parallels the structure of the decisions to be analyzed. The linear programming method was devised for this specific purpose.

The last few paragraphs have made use of a number of terms — linear programming, production process, factor, produce — without adequate definition. This was necessary in order to give some idea of the point of view taken by linear programming. Now we must proceed to a careful formulation of these concepts and to a statement of the linear programming approach to economic problems.

3. *Basic Concepts of Linear Programming*

Although this essay will be concerned chiefly with the application of linear programming to the theory of an individual firm, the technique itself has a much wider scope. Linear programming is basically the mathematical study of a certain kind of optimization, which we are about to describe, and applies whenever the facts of an economic situation fulfill, to a sufficiently good approximation, the mathematical postulates of the method. As a mathematical matter, linear programming has been defined to be the study of the maximization or minimization in the large of a mathematical function subject to linear inequalities. It differs, therefore, from the type of optimization treated in the calculus in three respects: first, it deals with optimization in the large, rather than in the small; second, it deals with restrictive inequalities, rather than with restrictive equalities; third, it deals with linear restrictions, rather than with restraints of more general form. Two of these differences are in the direction of making linear programming more general and more powerful than ordinary maximization, but the third is a restriction on its applicability, at least in the current state of its mathematical development.

Linear programming was developed in response to a specific economic problem, and it is not surprising therefore that there exists a considerable class of economic problems which fulfill its postulates. The particular problem which gave rise to linear programming may be expressed as follows. Consider a firm which has access to certain factors of production whose supply, for one reason or another, cannot be increased in the time period in view. These resources delimit the opportunities open to the firm. They may be utilized in various ways, or not at all, and depending on what is done with them the revenues, expenses, and profits of the firm will vary. The problem facing the management is to find the productive program which will make the profits of the firm as great as possible, subject to the limitation that this program must not require more than the total available supply of any resource. We must now consider how such a problem can be formulated so as to bring it within the scope of the mathematical theory of linear programming.

To do this we require three basic concepts: resources, products, and production processes. These three concepts cannot be defined without some circularity since they are defined in terms of each other, but this need not lead to confusion since the notions of resources and products are the same as those made familiar by the marginal analysis, and the concept of production processes, though not the same as that of the production function, is closely related to it.

A firm, even a retail store or a bank, is conceived of in economics as "an institution which buys things, transforms them in some way, and then sells them with the purpose of making a profit " (1, pp. 377). The things which a firm buys may, of course, be physical objects or they may be intangibles such as energy in any form, space, the services of a human being or animal, or the right to use some physical object for some period of time. We may think of all the physical and intangible things used by the firm as being grouped into classes in such a way that it is a matter of indifference to this firm or any firm which member of a class it obtains for use in its productive work. Such a class we shall call a resource, a factor, or an input. J. Robinson has expressed this same concept in somewhat more technical language, saying, ". . . the various elements required for the production of any commodity should be divided into groups, each group being a factor of production, in such a way that the elasticity of substitution between one factor and another is less than infinite" (31, pp. 330). Since each resource is a class of homogeneous elements, a measure of quantity can be found. Physical units — acres, kilowatts, tons, man-hours, dozen, and so forth — serve to measure the amounts of each resource consumed by a process of production.

The definition of a product or output is exactly similar. All the results of productive effort, whether physical or intangible, may be grouped into classes in such a way that any firm or individual desiring a member of a class would not care which member of that class he received. Such a class will be referred to as a product or a type of output and, like resources, to each product there corresponds an appropriate physical measure of quantity.

These two definitions are familiar. The definition of a productive process is somewhat novel. Essentially, a productive process is a physical event or series of events in which men participate purposefully in order to transform some resources into some products. Millions of such events take place daily, of course. Some are quite similar in the sense that they consume the same or similar resources and turn out the same or similar products, and some differ radically in their nature and purpose. Thus in defining a process a problem of classification arises. We shall say that two productive events are instances of the same process if they consume the same resources and in the same proportions, and if they produce the same outputs, and in the same proportions. Otherwise they are instances of different processes.

In order to avoid the chance of ambiguity inherent in any verbal definition which deals with quantitative matters we shall express our formal definition of a process algebraically, borrowing, for this purpose, chemical notation. Suppose that a certain productive event, which we shall denote by E_i, consumes m resources in various quantities and turns out n products in various quantities. We may express this as follows. Let the first factor be F_1 and the quantity consumed be a_{i1}, let the second factor be F_2 and the quantity consumed be a_{i2}, and so on. And let the first product be C_1 and the quantity produced be b_{i1}, the second product be C_2 and the quantity produced b_{i2}, etc. (Of course, the factors and products can be listed in any convenient order, alphabetical for example.) Then what has occurred is a transformation which may be written:

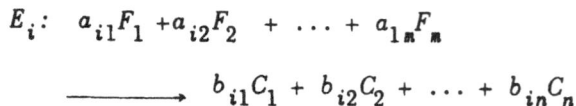

$$E_i: \quad a_{i1}F_1 + a_{i2}F_2 + \ldots + a_{1m}F_m$$
$$\longrightarrow \quad b_{i1}C_1 + b_{i2}C_2 + \ldots + b_{in}C_n$$

Suppose that there is another event, denoted by E_j, which consumes the same m resources and yields the same n products. This event may be described by:

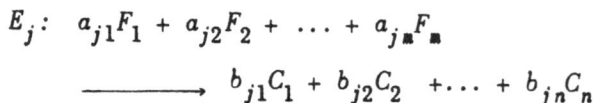

$$E_j: \quad a_{j1}F_1 + a_{j2}F_2 + \ldots + a_{jm}F_m$$
$$\longrightarrow \quad b_{j1}C_1 + b_{j2}C_2 + \ldots + b_{jn}C_n$$

Now if the inputs and outputs of these two processes are proportional throughout, that is if

$$a_{i1}/a_{j1} = a_{i2}/a_{j2} = a_{im}/a_{jm} = b_{i1}/b_{j1} = \ldots = b_{in}/b_{jn},$$

we shall say that the two events are instances of the same productive processes. Otherwise we shall regard them as instances of different productive processes, even though they make use of similar techniques and differ only in the ratios of the inputs and outputs. It is seen that, by definition, a process in this sense permits of only one type of variation, that of over-all scale.

A metric is therefore needed for describing the scale or intensity with which a process is carried on. All that is needed to provide such a scale is to select any instance of that process and define it as the unit level. Any other instance of the process will consume factors and yield products in some ratio to the unit level, and that unit may be used to measure the level of the process. For example, if E_i and E_j discussed above are instances of the same process, E_j may be selected as the unit level and then E_i will be at the level given by a_{i1}/a_{j1} or any of the other ratios. In such cases we shall make use of the notation:

$$E_i = (a_{i1}/a_{j1})E_j.$$

It is seen that the "process" of linear programming is a more specifically defined concept than the production function of the marginal analysis. Indeed, a production function is a family of processes which use the same factors and turn out the same products. If we compare any two points on a production surface, if the internal ratios of the inputs and outputs at the two points are the same they will represent different levels of the same process, otherwise they will represent different processes. The production function thus is a tool for exhibiting and comparing different but related processes. What it fails to present adequately is the consequence of using several processes in parallel, and such combinations of processes are characteristic of modern industry.

The reason for using combinations of processes is evident. As the output of any product or combination of products is increased the supply of the factors needed for the most efficient productive process will become exhausted. Then output can be expanded only by resorting to productive processes which make use of inferior resources or to processes which use the best resources in non-optimal ratios. As production increases, therefore, the common phenomenon of increasing costs is experienced because of recourse to more expensive processes. The average cost curve is a genuine average of the costs of all the processes which must be used to obtain a given output. This averaging is implicit in the conventional production function and cost curve, but quite explicit in the linear programming analysis. An example of this type of averaging would, perhaps, not be out of place.

Consider a firm which manufactures a single product and whose initial equipment consists in a plant with a capacity of 100 units of output per hour, stand-by equipment with a capacity of 25 units per hour, and a trained staff adequate to operate the main plant. Let us suppose that direct material cost is $0.50 per unit for production in the main plant and $0.55 per unit for production in the stand-by plant and that direct labor cost is $0.60 per unit in the main plant using trained personnel. If stand-by equipment is to be used, the inferiority of both the equipment and the personnel will combine to raise direct labor cost to, say, $0.70 per unit produced on stand-by equipment even though hourly wage rates remain the same. Both the main plant and the stand-by equipment can be operated up to fifty hours a month at overtime wage rates, which are 150 per cent of regular wage rates. We shall neglect the firm's fixed costs since these will be incurred in any case and will not influence production decisions. The word "costs" in the next few paragraphs will therefore mean variable costs.

Let us now trace this firm's average cost curve. Assuming a normal work-month of 176 hours, the firm can produce up to 17,600 units at a constant average (and marginal) cost of $1.10 per unit. If production is to go beyond 17,600 units, stand-by facilities can be used at a unit cost of $1.25 until an output of 22,000 units has been reached. Production can be pushed up to 27,000 units per month by using the normal equipment and staff on overtime, at a unit cost of $1.40 for the last 5,000 units. And finally, the stand-by plant can be used on overtime to produce 1,250 additional units at a cost of $1.60 each. There are other possibilities too, for example multiple shift operation, but these will suffice to bring out the major characteristics of the situation.

The average cost curve generated by these conditions is as follows. For the first 17,600 units the average unit cost is constant
at $1.10. Thereafter, until 22,000 units are reached, the average
cost is given by

Average cost = $1.25 - 2,640/x$ where x = output in units.

For output between 22,000 and 27,000 units we have:

Average cost = $1.40 - 5,940/x$.

And finally, for output between 27,000 and 28,250 units,

Average cost = $1.60 - 11,340/x$.

This curve is shown in figure 1. In broad outline it follows the
usual concept of a cost curve rising with increasing steepness,
but examined in detail it displays discontinuities in its derivatives whenever new production conditions have to be introduced.

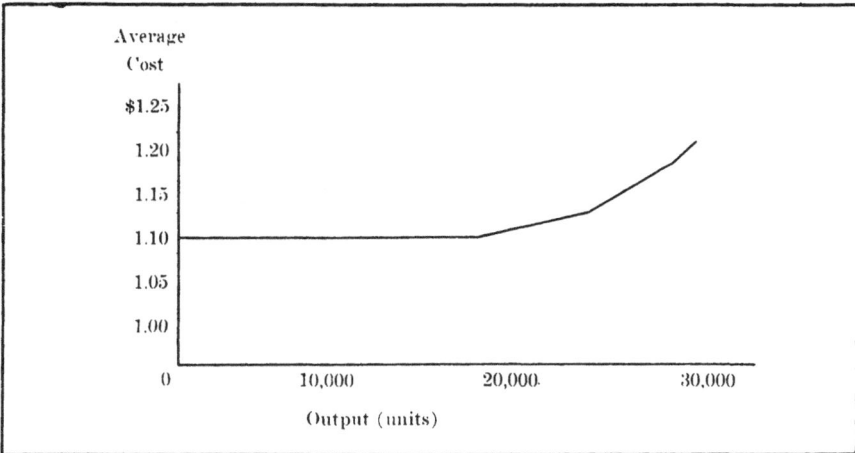

Fig. 1. Average cost curve for firm in pure competition.

In this example the only limitation on the operation of the
firm arose from its limited supply of installed equipment, and
the need for combining processes arose when the desired output
became out of balance with the capacity of this equipment. In

chapter ii we shall study cases in which the operations of a firm are subject to several restrictions. In such cases the need for combining several processes will be seen to arise from somewhat different considerations.

To some extent the apparent divergence between linear programming and more familiar modes of analysis arises from differences in the manner of expressing the same phenomenon. Consider, for example, telephone calls, which may be switched either by human switchboard operators or by automatic (dial) selectors. If a telephone central changes over from the human to the automatic system, the marginal analysis would describe the change as an increase in the ratio of capital equipment to human inputs, while linear programming would describe the same event as a decrease in the level of one process, human switching, compensated by an increase in the level of another process, automatic switching. In analyzing switchboard operations, the marginal technique would be concerned with finding the optimum ratio of capital equipment to human operators without explicit consideration of the technical methods for achieving this optimum. Linear programming, by contrast, would search explicitly for the optimum level of each method of operation without explicit consideration of the ratios of different inputs on a system-wide basis. Which approach is more relevant, of course, depends on the problem in hand.

We may now state the basic assumptions of linear programming. They are:

1. The productive opportunities of an economy or economic unit are defined by the resources and the productive processes available to it. The quantities of at least some of the resources are finite and so is the number of productive processes available.

2. Any productive process may be used at any positive level consistent with the supply of resources available. The consumption of resources and the output of products is proportional to the level at which the process is used.

3. Several productive processes may be used simultaneously, if the supply of resources is adequate. If this is done, the consumption of each resource is the sum of the consumptions of the individual processes used, and the output of products is the sum of the outputs of the individual processes..

Within this framework, the productive problem becomes the problem of choosing which productive processes to use and the level at which to use each of them. It will be useful to formulate this problem algebraically.

We shall make use of the concept of the production program, denoted by T, which is simply the totality of all the productive processes used by the firm. A productive process, in turn, is completely specified by giving the quantities of each of the inputs which it consumes and each of the outputs which it produces when carried on at unit level. Thus the process denoted above by E_j can be written more briefly as

$$E_j = (a_{j1} \ a_{j2} \ \cdots \ a_{jm} \ b_{j1} \ b_{j2} \ \cdots \ b_{jn}),$$

it being easily understood which factor or product each of the coefficients refers to. Expressions of this type will occur frequently in the treatment and, unless otherwise noted, will be regarded as column vectors. A production program, T, made up of the processes P_1, P_2, $\ldots$, P_k is simply the sum of the vectors of the several processes, each being taken at the level at which it occurs in the program. Thus if P_1 is used at level x_1, P_2 at level x_2, etc., then

$$T = x_1 P_1 + x_2 P_2 + \ldots + x_k P_k.$$

The program is completely specified by the vector, X, of process intensities, that is, by

$$X = (x_1 \ x_2 \ \cdots \ x_k).$$

The inputs and outputs of the production program T can now be expressed in terms of the corresponding process intensity vector, X. Let

$$P_1 = (a_{i1} \ a_{i2} \ \cdots \ a_{im} \ b_{i1} \ b_{i2} \ \cdots \ b_{in}), \quad (i = 1, \ 2, \ \ldots, \ k)$$

and let z_1 denote the consumption of the first factor, z_2 the consumption of the second factor, and so on. Then, clearly

$$Z_1 = a_{11} x_1 + a_{21} x_2 + \ldots + a_{k1} x_k,$$

$$Z_2 = a_{12} x_1 + a_{22} x_2 + \ldots + a_{k2} x_k, \quad etc.$$

If we write, for compactness:

$$A_i = (a_{i1} \ a_{i2} \ \cdots \ a_{im}), \quad \text{(a column vector)}$$

$$A = (A_1 \ A_2 \ \cdots \ A_k), \quad \begin{array}{l} \text{a matrix of } m \text{ rows and} \\ k \text{ columns,} \end{array}$$

$$Z = (z_1 \ z_2 \ \cdots \ z_m)$$

then

$$Z = AX$$

expresses the inputs required by the production program.

Now if there are s_1 units of the first resource available, s_2 units of the second resource, and so forth, and if

$$S = (s_1 \ s_2 \ \cdots \ s_m)$$

then the resource limitation can be expressed by the requirement that all production programs must satisfy the inequality:

$$AX < S$$

The output side is treated similarly. Let y_1 be the output of the first product, y_2 the output of the second product, and so on, and define:

$$Y = (y_1 \ y_2 \ \cdots \ y_n)$$

$$B_i = (b_{i1} \ b_{i2} \ \cdots \ b_{in})$$

$$B = (B_1 \ B_2 \ \cdots \ B_k).$$

Then, just as for the inputs,

$$Y = BX$$

Now the valuation placed by a society or other unit of decision on a production program is a function of the inputs of resources, the outputs of products, and perhaps the process intensities themselves. We have just seen that the inputs and outputs may be expressed in terms of the process intensities, so the measure of desirability of a production program is some function of the process intensity vector, say $f(X)$. Then the basic problem of linear programming is simply to find the intensity vector

X to which corresponds the largest attainable measure of desirability, $f(X)$ subject to the limitations

$\quad\quad X > 0$ $\quad\quad$ (No process can be used at negative level.)

$\quad\quad AX < S$ $\quad\quad$ (No more resources can be used than are available.)

It should be noted that this formulation will frequently not serve to define a unique optimum program because there may be several programs whose measures of desirability, $f(X)$, are equal or, as is frequent in analysis of social optima, non-comparable. Non-comparability has been studied intensively by Koopmans (20), but will not concern us in applying linear programming to the theory of the firm since we can adopt a one-dimensional measure of desirability, namely profitability.

The concepts which have been advanced thus far are adequate as theoretical tools, but their applicability to the phenomenal world requires slight amplification.

The definitions of resource and product required absolute homogeneity within each class. If an attempt were made to apply these concepts strictly to any practical firm or problem, the analysis would have to be carried out in terms of a prohibitively large number of resources, processes, and products. But, of course, a theory can be applied usefully to a practical context which it describes only approximately. Thus in a practical context, theoretically heterogeneous units may be lumped into a practically homogeneous class and treated as if they were to all intents and purposes homogeneous. Indeed, one of the early great achievements in linear programming, that of Leontief (23), consisted in describing the structure of American industry in terms of only some forty processes and products each of which, for the purposes in hand, could be considered homogeneous. As a practical matter, then homogeneity is relative to the problem under consideration.

There is still one ambiguity in the concept of a process which remains to be cleared up. Nearly all products pass through a number of successive stages in their process of manufacture. For example, the manufacture of a book involves first typesetting

and then printing and finally binding, and each of these stages
can be broken down still further if desired. What then is a process? Is it book manufacture, or is it typesetting, or is it
carrying type from the machine to the galley-form? The answer to
this depends on the nature of the problem in hand. Clearly if it
is desirable to consider the relationships of sub-processes it
will be convenient to define them individually. On the other
hand if interest focuses on the larger processes and the relationships of the component operations can be assumed to be established
it will, in general, be most practical to use the notion of
the process to denote the largest series of operations for which
the ratios of the first inputs to the last outputs are rigidly
determined.

- - - - - - - - - - - - - - - - -

The Competitive Firm
Using Fixed Factors

1. *Formulation of the Problem*

We may think of an entrepreneur at the beginning of a production planning period as having certain fixed factors of production at his disposal and as having access to competitive markets in which he can procure the variable factors needed to make use of his fixed factors. His problem is essentially to devise a production program which will utilize the fixed factors to best advantage, that is, secure the greatest possible profit from their use. To a farmer, for example, the controlling fixed factor is land of given characteristics and his production program consists of decisions as to crops and methods and intensities of cultivation. A chemical firm, similarly, inherits a fixed plant of given characteristics from previous production periods and often has a considerable latitude in selecting the end products it is to produce and the raw materials and processes to be used. It would be hard to imagine a firm which does not periodically face this problem of finding the optimum use for its inherited equipment.

In order to characterize the situation more precisely, we shall assume that the firm has n factors, which are not perfect substitutes for each other, in fixed supply. We shall assume also that there are k processes, each of which uses at least one of these factors, available to the firm. Thus the problem is that of deciding which of the k available processes are to be used at all, and the level at which each is to be carried on.

Generally speaking, each of the k available processes will use some of the fixed factors, the quantity depending on the level at which the process is carried on and on the nature of the process, and will use also some variable factors which must be purchased on the open market. A process will result in the production of salable commodities, and we shall assume that these are to be sold under competitive conditions. The excess of the revenue resulting from the sale of the commodities produced by a process over the cost of the variable factors required will be referred to as the net revenue of that process. A process may therefore be characterized by the quantity of each of the fixed factors which is required in order that that process be carried on at a level which results in a net revenue of \$1. Symbolically, we shall denote a process by a column vector such as:

$$P_i = (a_{i1} \quad a_{i2} \quad \cdots \quad a_{in})$$

$$i = 1, 2, \ldots, k.$$

where a_{ij} is the consumption of the jth fixed factor by one unit of the ith process.

(Prime marks (′) throughout this chapter will indicate transposed vectors and matrices.) We shall denote by x_i the level at which the ith process is used. In consequence of these definitions, if process P_i is used at level x_i it will yield a net revenue of $\$x_i$ and will consume $x_i a_{i1}$ units of the first limited factor, $x_i a_{i2}$ units of the second limited factor, and so on.

In general, a firm may use several processes at various levels. It may use Process 1 at level x_1 Process 2 at level x_2 and so on. In this case, the aggregate net revenue will be the sum of the net revenues of the individual processes, or:

$$r = x_1 + x_2 + \ldots + x_k.$$

In this formula, it should be remarked, some of the x's may be zero. Similarly, the aggregate consumption of each of the limited factors is the sum of the quantities consumed by each of the k processes. This may be written:

$$Z = x_1 P_1 + x_2 P_2 + \ldots + x_k P_k.$$

It will be most convenient to use this formula in matrix form. We note that each of the P_i is a column vector of n elements, so that

$$A = (P_1 \ P_2 \ \ldots \ P_k)$$

is a matrix of n rows and k columns. We can denote the production program by a k-element column vector,

$$X = (x_1 \ x_2 \ \ldots \ x_k)$$

where the ith element denotes the level at which the ith process is operated. Given such a production program vector, X the total consumption of the n limited factors, may be written

$$Z = AX$$

and the total resultant net revenue may be written

$$r = 1'X$$

where $1'$ is a row vector consisting of k ones.

At this stage the maximizing problem faced by the firm can be formulated as follows: Suppose that the firm has available S_1 units of the first limited factor, S_2 units of the second limited factor, $\ldots$, S_m units of the nth and last limited factor. And let

$$S = (S_1 \ S_2 \ \ldots \ S_n).$$

Then the firm must attempt to maximize

$$r = 1'X$$

subject to the restrictions

$$X > 0$$

$$AX < S$$

The problem is, however, not very convenient to solve in the form just stated, and will now be reformulated by means of a device for which Dr. George B. Dantzig is responsible. This device consists in the introduction of "disposal processes." It will be assumed that if the production plan does not make use of the entire available supply of one or more of the limited factors, the excess will go costlessly to waste. We shall introduce n

"disposal processes," one for each limited factor, and shall denote them by P_{k+1}, P_{k+2}, . . ., P_{k+n} where P_{k+j} is the process of allowing one unit of the jth limited factor to go to waste. In vector form, the disposal processes may be written:

$$P_{k+1} = (1 \ 0 \ 0 \ \ldots \ 0)'$$

$$P_{k+2} = (0 \ 1 \ 0 \ \ldots \ 0)'$$

$$\ldots \ldots \ldots \ldots \ldots \ldots \ldots \ldots$$

$$P_{k+n} = (0 \ 0 \ 0 \ \ldots \ 1)'$$

Now we may think of the firm as having $k+n$ processes — k active and n disposal — available to it. Its production program vector will therefore have $k+n$ elements, that is:

$$X = (x_1 \ x_2 \ \ldots \ x_{k+n}).$$

The matrix of production possibilities will have to be expanded to have $k+n$ columns. It becomes:

$$B = (P_1 \ P_2 \ \ldots \ P_{k+n}) = (A \ I)$$

where I is the identity matrix of n rows and columns.

The formula for net revenue also has to be altered. We introduce the column vector

$$V = (v_1 \ v_2 \ \ldots \ v_{k+n})$$

where:

$$v_i = \begin{cases} 1 \text{ if } P_i \text{ is an active process} \\ 0 \text{ if } P_i \text{ is a disposal process.} \end{cases}$$

This vector, of course, represents the net revenue resulting from the use of one unit of each of the $k+n$ available processes. Then aggregate net revenue is:

$$r = V'X$$

Throughout the rest of the chapter we shall always include disposal processes when we talk of production processes or production programs. The maximizing problem now takes the following form:

$$r = V'X \text{ is to be maximized}$$

subject to restrictions:

$$X \geq O$$
$$BX = S$$

The advantage of this over the previous formulation is that an equality has replaced the inequality in the second restriction.

2. *The Basic Theorem*

Our discussion of this maximizing problem will be based on the theory of linear programming devised largely by Dantzig (6 and 8). We make three additional assumptions regarding the problem:

1. Every sub-set of n processes, P_i, forms a linearly independent set of vectors.

2. Every sub-set of $n+1$ vectors $(v_i \ P_i')$ is a linearly independent set.

3. The vector S which specifies the available quantities of the limited factors, is linearly independent of every set of n-1 processes.

The meaning and consequences of these assumptions will be discussed more fully later on. For the present just one comment need be made. If any process uses only one scarce factor its vector will be linearly dependent on the vector for the disposal process for that factor. This disposal process is then otiose and should be omitted from the schedule of available processes.

As a consequence of assumption 1, every set of n process vectors forms an $n \times n$ matrix of rank n. We shall also have occasion to use the enlarged matrix

$$\begin{pmatrix} V' \\ B \end{pmatrix}$$

whose ith column is $(v_i \ P_i')'$. This matrix has $n+1$ rows and k

columns. It is of rank $n+1$ by assumption 2.

We now note that there exists a solution to

$$BX = S$$

in which no more than n elements of X are positive, the rest being zero. For example, the vector

$$X = (O' \; S')'$$

where O' denotes a row of k zeros

clearly satisfies the equation since

$$B \begin{pmatrix} O \\ S \end{pmatrix} = (A \; I) \begin{pmatrix} O \\ S \end{pmatrix} = IS = S.$$

A solution in which no more than n elements of X enter with positive values will be referred to as basic solution. The n process vectors which enter into a basic solution with positive multipliers will be called the basis corresponding to that solution. We have already produced one basic solution. There will, in general, be many of them; others can be found readily by selecting any active process and any $n-1$ disposal processes.

By reason of assumption 3, all basic solutions involve precisely n elements of X at positive values, for otherwise S would be linearly dependent on the fewer-than-n processes whose vectors had positive weights in the solution. The economic meaning of the existence of basic solutions, which has just been shown, is that no matter what bill of supplies of n scarce factors is available, a production schedule using just n processes (including disposal processes) can be constructed which will utilize them all.

We are now in a position to state the basic theorem of linear programming: The solution which maximizes aggregate net revenue is a basic solution.

We shall prove this by assuming that the theorem is not true and thereby forcing a contradiction. Let the maximizing solution be X, so that:

$$r = V'X = \text{maximum}$$
$$BX = S$$

Let X have t positive components where $t > n$. Without loss of generality we can assume that the processes have been numbered in such a way that the first t elements of X are the positive ones. We now partition the B and X matrices as follows: Let

B_1 be the first n columns of B

B_2 be the next $t-n$ columns of B

B_3 be the last $k+n-t$ columns of B

X_1 be the first n elements of X

X_2 be the next $t-n$ elements of X

X_3 be the last $k+n-t$ elements of X

The elements of X_3 are all zero.

Then by hypothesis:

$$(B_1 \; B_2 \; B_3) \begin{pmatrix} X_1 \\ X_2 \\ X_3 \end{pmatrix} = (B_1 \; B_2) \begin{pmatrix} X_1 \\ X_2 \end{pmatrix} = S,$$

$$B_1 X_1 + B_2 X_2 = S,$$

$$X_1, \; X_2 > 0$$

By assumption 1, B_1 is a non-singular square matrix. We may therefore write:

$$X_1 = B_1^{-1} S - B_1^{-1} B_2 X_2.$$

For convenience, let

$$Q = B_1^{-1} B_2 \text{ and } Q_0 = B_1^{-1} S$$

Then

$$X_1 = Q_0 - QX_2$$

Now it is necessary to bring the net revenue function into the picture. We partition the unit net revenue vector, V, to correspond to the partitioning of X and write:

$$r = V'X = V_1'X_1 + V_2'X_2.$$

Using the expression for X_1 in terms of X_2 we have:

$$r = V_1'Q_0 + (V_2' - V_1'Q) X_2.$$

Since $X_1, X_2 > 0$ we can vary each component of X_2 slightly both upward and downward without forcing any element of X_1 or X_2 to vanish or become negative. Now we have assumed that r is as great as possible, so that no such variation can increase it. This can happen only if:

$$V_2' - V_1'Q = 0$$

or

$$V_2' = V_1'Q.$$

Now, obviously,
$$B_2 = B_1 Q.$$

Thus we see that the $(n+1) \times t$ matrix

$$\begin{pmatrix} V_1' & V_2' \\ B_1 & B_2 \end{pmatrix}$$

is of rank n. But this contradicts assumption 2. Therefore we cannot have $t > n$, and the theorem is proved.

We have now shown that the optimum production schedule, under the assumptions given, will involve exactly n production processes at positive levels. Some of these may be disposal processes, of course

3. *Computational Procedure*

It will be instructive to present a computational procedure for finding the optimum production program. This procedure will be iterative. It will consist in starting with any basic solution and deriving from it another basic solution which is more profitable. The procedure is repeated until no further improvement is possible.

It is easy to find a starting point. As was mentioned, a production program made up of the n disposal processes will do. As a practical matter, however, it will generally be better to start with a program which consists of one active process plus n-1 disposal processes.

Now it is necessary to show how, given any basic solution, a better basic solution can be derived from it unless the solution at hand is already optimal. Let X be a basic solution, that is, let X satisfy:

$$BX = S,$$

$$X \geq 0.$$

Exactly n components of X are positive, the rest being zero. Without loss of generality we can assume that the processes have been numbered in such a way that the first n elements of X are the positive ones. Then we can partition B after the nth column and X after the nth element and write:

$$B_1 X_1 + B_2 X_2 = S.$$

Since B_1 is non-singular by assumption 1, we can solve this for X_1, obtaining:

$$X_1 = B_1^{-1} S - B_1^{-1} B_2 X_2.$$

Let

$$Q = B_1^{-1} B_2, \text{ and } Q_0 = B_1^{-1} S.$$

We have:

$$X_1 = Q_0 - QX_2.$$

The unit profit vector, V, can be partitioned correspondingly, giving:

$$r = V_1' \, X_1 + V_2' \, X_2$$

$$= V_1' \, B_1^{-1} \, S + (V_2' - V_1' \, Q) \, X_2$$

$$= V_1' \, Q_0 + (V_2' - V_1' \, Q) \, X_2 \, .$$

So far we have assumed $X_2 = 0$. Since $X_1 > 0$, each component of X_2 can be increased at least slightly without forcing any component of X_1 to become zero or negative.

Now if

$$V_2' - V_1' \, Q < 0$$

an increase in any component in X_2 will decrease net revenue if the inequality holds for that component or will leave net revenue unchanged if the equality holds.[1] At any rate, no change in X_2 will increase revenue and the production schedule denoted by X is optimal.

We shall refer to the inequality

$$V_2' - V_1' Q < 0$$

as the "simplex criterion," and any set of n process vectors which leads to matrices which satisfy the inequality will be said to satisfy the simplex criterion. We have just seen that a basis which satisfies the simplex criterion corresponds to an optimum production plan.

On the other hand if the simplex criterion is not satisfied, that is, if there is a positive element in $(V_2' - V_1'Q)$ then it will be possible to increase r by giving a positive value to at least one component of X_2 Thus if assumptions 1 and 2 hold, satisfaction of the simplex criterion is a necessary and sufficient condition for a basic solution to be optimal.

Now let us consider the situation which arises when one or more of the elements of $(V_2' - V_1'Q)$ are positive. To do this we

---

[1] It may be noted that by reason of assumption 2 the equality never actually occurs.

shall have to look more closely at the matrices which enter into r. They are:

$$V_1' = (v_1 \ v_2 \ \cdots \ v_n),$$

$$V_2' = (v_{n+1} \ v_{n+2} \ \cdots \ v_{n+k}),$$

$$B_1 = (P_1 \ P_2 \ \cdots \ P_n),$$

$$B_2 = (P_{n+i} \ P_{n+2} \ \cdots \ P_{n+k}),$$

$$Q = B_1^{-1} \ B_2.$$

We shall number the columns of Q to correspond to the columns of B_2, so that we write:

$$Q = (Q_{n+1} \ Q_{n+2} \ \cdots \ Q_{n+k} \ )$$

where Q_{n+i} is the n-element column vector which is a solution to the equation

$$(P_1 \ P_2 \ \cdots \ P_n) \ Q_{n+i} = P_{n+i}$$

Thus Q_{n+i} is the vector which specifies the combination of the n processes in the basis which consumes the same quantities of the limited factors as P_{n+i}. We shall therefore refer to Q_{n+i} as the equivalent combination to P_{n+i}.

The profit resulting from process P_{n+i} at unit level is, by definition, V_{n+i}. The profit resulting from the equivalent combination is, clearly:

$$V_1' \ Q_{n+i}.$$

Now let us consider the vector $(V_2' - V_1' \ Q)$.

It can be written:

$$(V_2' - V_1' \ Q) = (v_{n+1} \ v_{n+2} \ \cdots \ v_{n+k}) - V_1' \ (Q_{n+1} \ Q_{n+2} \ \cdots \ Q_{n+k})$$

$$= (v_{n+1} - V_1' Q_{n+1} \ \ v_{n+2} - V_1' Q_{n+2} \ \cdots \ v_{n+k} - V_1' \ Q_{n+k})$$

If each of these elements is negative, it signifies that each process excluded from the basis is less profitable than the equivalent combination which consumes the same quantities of the limited factors. Thus the simplex criterion asserts that a basis is optimal if and only if no excluded process is more profitable than the equivalent combination formed from processes in that basis.

Now, if

$$v_{n+i} - V_1' Q_{n+i} > 0$$

it is seen from the net revenue equation that net revenue can be increased by taking x_{n+i} in X_2 greater than zero. Indeed, the larger x_{n+i} is, the larger net revenue will be. But there is a limitation on how large x_{n+i} can be permitted to become, since as x_{n+i} grows some or all of the components of X_1 decrease and x_{n+i} is limited by the fact that none of these components can be allowed to become negative. Then if all the elements of X_2 are zero except x_{n+i},

$$X_1 = Q_0 - x_{n+i} Q_{n+i}.$$

Denote the components of Q_0 by q_{oj} and those of Q_{n+i} by $q_{n+i,j}$ where $j = 1, 2, \ldots, n$. Then:

$$x_j = q_{oj} - x_{n+i} q_{n+i,j}.$$

Then x_{n+i} can be permitted to increase until the first of the x_j vanishes. Suppose x_p is the first one to vanish, that is, suppose

$$\frac{q_{op}}{q_{n+i,p}} = \text{minimum}_j \left(\frac{q_{oj}}{q_{n+i,j}} \right), \text{taken over all } j \text{ for which } q_{n+i,j} > 0.$$

Then the maximum permissable value of x_{n+i} is:

$$x_{n+i} = \frac{q_{op}}{q_{n+i,p}}.$$

Now, let all the elements of X_2 remain zero except X_{n+i} which takes the value just found. Net revenue becomes:

$$r_1 = V_1' Q_0 + (v_{n+i} - V_1' Q_{n+i}) \frac{q_{op}}{q_{n+i,p}}.$$

Since the parenthesis is positive, r_1 is clearly greater than r. What has happened is that P_p has been removed from the basis,

P_{n+i} has been added to it, and a new basic solution has been generated from the old one with a concomitant increase in profits. This procedure of altering the basis can be applied over and over until a basic solution is found which satisfies the optimality condition.

We have now found a procedure for beginning with any basic solution and altering it step by step until the optimum production program has been found. This optimum program will include just n processes and will have the property that no excluded process is more profitable than the equivalent combination of included processes.

4. *The Three Assumptions*

The results established thus far have depended on three restrictive assumptions. It is now necessary to consider the roles played by these assumptions in the development and the consequences of relaxing them. The assumptions will be discussed in numerical order.

Consider first the case in which assumption 1 is violated but assumptions 2 and 3 are still satisfied. To be specific let

$$\text{Rank} \quad (B_1) \, < \, n,$$

where B_1 is defined as in the preceding discussion, while, because of assumption 3,

$$\text{Rank} \quad (B_1 \, S) = n$$

Then the system of linear equations

$$B_1 \, X_1 = S$$

is inconsistent. From this it follows that a set of n processes the matrix of whose vectors is singular cannot constitute a solution of the maximizing problem. Such a set will not be selected as a starting point for the iterative process nor will the iterative process ever generate such a set since the bases generated by the iterative process are necessarily solutions of the equation system. Finally, the exclusion of such sets from the iterative process is no loss since they are not solutions at all and therefore cannot be optimum solutions.

The purpose of this assumption in the development was to guarantee that the matrix B_1 of the basic solution being considered could be inverted. Now it is seen that this guarantee can be met on the basis of a much weaker condition, namely that the production possibility matrix, B, be of rank n, that is, that there exist at least one n-column non-singular submatrix in B. This condition will always be met since B contains a sub-set of columns which form the identity matrix or at least a diagonal matrix.

Assumption 2, also, is not critical. This assumption was used to prove the theorem that the optimum solution to a production problem with n factors in limited supply involves n production processes. If the assumption is not satisfied, there may be an optimal production program involving more than n processes but, in this event, there will also be a program involving only n processes which will yield the same net revenue. Thus the optimum basic solution, which can be discovered by means of the iterative procedure, yields as much net revenue as any possible solution and the iterative procedure can be relied on.

To show this it is necessary to prove the following theorem: If there exists a maximizing solution to the production problem in which t processes are involved at positive levels, $t > n$, then there also exists a solution involving only n processes at positive levels which yields the maximum net revenue. We shall assume that

$$\text{Rank} \quad (P_1 \; P_2 \; \ldots \; P_t) = n$$

Let

$$R_1^* = (v_i \; P_i') = (v_i \; a_{i1} \; a_{i2} \; \ldots \; a_{in})'$$

Assume for definiteness that the t processes involved in the maximizing solution are the first t and that the resulting net revenue is r. Then, the solution is the vector

$$X = (x_1 \; x_2 \; \ldots \; x_t)'$$

such that

(1.1) $$x_1 P_1^* + x_2 P_2^* + \ldots + x_n P_n^* + \ldots + x_t P_t^* = \binom{r}{S}$$

We have already found, in the proof of the main theorem, that if r is the maximum obtainable net revenue then each of the processes

P_{n+1}^*, P_{n+2}^*, $\ldots$, P_t^* is linearly dependent on the first n processes. Thus there exists a set of multipliers, w_1, w_2, $\ldots$, w_n, w_t, such that

$$(1.2) \qquad w_1 P_1^* + w_2 P_2^* + \ldots + w_n P_n^* + w_t P_t^* = 0.$$

Let ϕ be defined by

$$\phi = \min_i \quad \frac{x_i}{w_i} \quad , \quad i = 1, 2, \ldots, n, t.$$

and let p equal the value of i for which the minimum occurs. Multiply equation (1.2) by ϕ and subtract from equation (1.1) to obtain:

$$(x_1 - \phi w_1) P_1^* + (x_2 - \phi w_2) P_2^* + \ldots + 0 \, P_p^* + \ldots$$

$$+ (x_n - \phi w_n) P_n^* + (x_t - \phi w_t) P_t^* = \binom{r}{s}$$

We have now found a solution which involves at most t-1 processes with positive weights and which yields the same net revenue as the t-process solution with which we started. If the number of processes remaining with positive weights is still greater than n, this procedure can be repeated until finally only n processes remain. Thus there exists a basic solution which yields as great a net revenue as the best non-basic solution. Assumption 2 is consequently inessential from the point of view of computation, although its absence forces the modification of the basic theorem.

Finally it is necessary to consider assumption 3. If this assumption does not hold S is linearly dependent on some sub-set of less than n columns of B. A solution may then exist which involves less than n processes, and this solution may be optimal.

Let us assume that by the iterative procedure or other means we have arrived at a basic solution in which t processes occur with positive weights, $t < n$. To these t processes add n-t additional processes so as to obtain an n-process basic solution. Although this basis now consists, formally, of n processes, only t of them, of course, are used at positive levels in the corresponding production plan. Assume that the matrix of this solution, B_1, is non-singular. Then we have, just as before:

$$B_1 X_1 + B_2 X_2 = S,$$
$$X_1 = B_1^{-1} S - Q X_2,$$
$$r = V_1' B_1^{-1} S + (V_2' - V_1' Q) X_2.$$

In these equations, however, some of the elements of X_1 are zero when $X_2 = 0$. Two situations can now arise. First, suppose $V_2' - V_1' Q \leq 0$. Then an increase above zero of any element of X_2 would cause a decrease or at best no change in net revenue. Thus we can assert that even in the absence of assumption 3 the simplex criterion is a sufficient condition for the solution to be optimal.

Second, suppose that for some number p, $n < p < n+k$

$$v_p - V_1' Q_p > 0.$$

Let

$$X_2 = (\, 0 \; 0 \; \ldots \; x_p \; \ldots \; 0)\,'.$$

Then

$$X_1 = Q_0 - Q_p x_p,$$

$$r = V_1' Q_0 + (v_p - V_1' Q_p) x_p,$$

where, as before

$$Q_0 = B_1^{-1} S.$$

Under these circumstances it would be desirable to introduce into the production program the process corresponding to x_p. But this may not be possible since x_p cannot exceed

$$x_p = \text{minimum } i \; \frac{q_{0i}}{q_{pi}}, \; i = 1, 2, \ldots, n$$

and this minimum may be zero. If, then, a solution which involves fewer than n processes fails to meet the optimality criteria, that solution may still be optimum. That is, if assumption 3 is not satisfied, the simplex criterion is no longer a necessary condition of optimality.

Although the author and others have devoted considerable attention to the problem, no satisfactory criterion for optimality has yet been discovered for the case where the vector of

factor availabilities is linearly dependent on $n-1$ or fewer process vectors. It may be conjectured on the basis of present knowledge and some empirical trials that if the computations are carried out as if assumption 3 were satisfied, then an optimum solution will be obtained in a finite number of steps whether or not
assumption 3 is in fact satisfied. In other words, all current
methods of proof break down in the absence of assumption 3, but
the theorems appear to be true nevertheless. Establishment of
these assertions is one of the important current problems in the
mathematical theory of linear programming.

5. *Firm with Two Fixed Factors*

The foregoing discussion has been couched in very general terms
which, perhaps, makes it difficult to comprehend the economic
significance of the relationships and concepts which have been
arrived at. It will be instructive, therefore, to apply our results to a relatively simple case, that of a firm with two fixed
factors; that is, a firm for which $n = 2$. For concreteness we
shall assume that this firm has five productive processes among
which to choose.

The alternatives open to such a firm may be shown on a graph,
as in figure 2. In figure 2, each of the points P_1, P_2, ... P_5
represents a process at unit level. For example, if Process 1 is
used in sufficient amount so that a net revenue of \$1 is obtained,
it will require a_{11} units of Factor 1 and a_{12} units of Factor 2.

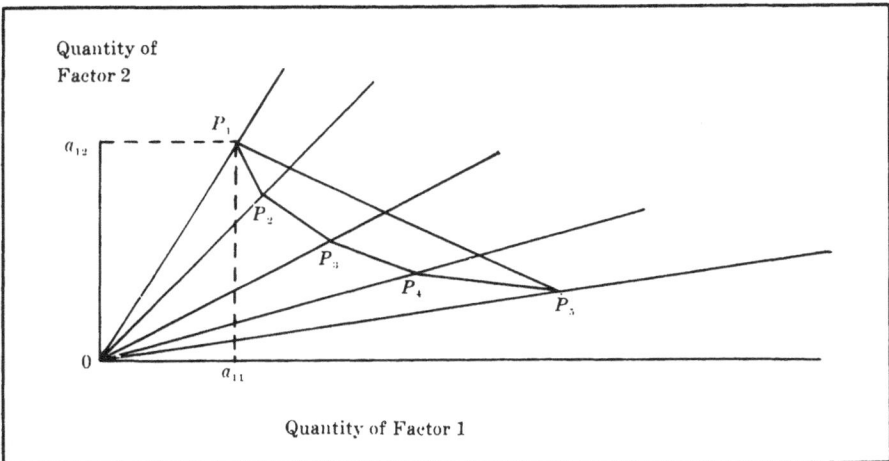

Fig. 2. *Production opportunities, two factor case.*

This is represented by point P_1 in the figure. Each of the other processes is represented similarly by a point whose coördinates are the quantities of the two fixed factors which are required in order to obtain a net revenue of $1 from its use.

Consider now the radius vector, or ray, through P_1. If Process 1 is carried on at the level represented by P_1 it will use up quantities a_{11} and a_{12}, respectively, of the two fixed factors and will return a net revenue of $1. Now it is assumed that by purchasing different quantities of variable factors (not shown in the figure) this process can be carried on at any level so long as it does not require more than the total available supply of either of the fixed factors. Since whatever the level of Process 1 it will consume the two fixed factors in the ratio of a_{11} units of Factor 1 to a_{12} units of Factor 2, the radius vector through P_1 represents all the possible quantities of the two fixed factors which will be required as Process 1 is employed to a greater or lesser extent. Each point on the radius vector corresponds to a different net revenue, of course, since the net revenue is proportional to the consumption of fixed factors, the ratio of proportionality being $1 of net revenue for a_{11} units consumed of Factor 1 or a_{12} units of Factor 2. The radius vectors through the other process points describe in a similar manner the way in which the quantities consumed of the two fixed factors depend on the level at which each process is used.

In the diagram chords have been drawn to connect neighboring process points and also P_1 and P_5. The significance of these chords can be seen by studying, for example, the one connecting P_1 and P_5. Let us consider a production program which utilizes only Processes 1 and 5. If it uses x_1 units of Process 1 and x_5 units of Process 5 it may be written as

$$T = x_1 P_1 + x_5 P_5$$

and the aggregate net revenue will be

$$r = x_1 + x_5.$$

Let us consider all production plans of this type such that $r = 1$, so that
$$x_5 = 1 - x_1.$$

Then:

$$T = x_1 P_1 + (1-x_1) P_5 = \begin{pmatrix} a_{11} & a_{51} \\ \\ a_{12} & a_{52} \end{pmatrix} \begin{pmatrix} x_1 \\ \\ 1-x_1 \end{pmatrix}$$

Denoting T by the vector

$$T = \begin{pmatrix} a_1 \\ a_2 \end{pmatrix}$$

we have:

$$\begin{pmatrix} a_1 \\ \\ a_2 \end{pmatrix} = \begin{pmatrix} a_{51} + (a_{11} - a_{51})x_1 \\ \\ a_{52} + (a_{12} - a_{52})x_1 \end{pmatrix}$$

Eliminating x_1 from these equations:

$$\frac{a_1 - a_{51}}{a_2 - a_{52}} = \frac{a_{11} - a_{51}}{a_{12} - 52},$$

which shows that the point (a_1, a_2) lies on the straight line through P_1 and P_5. We may thus say, in general, that the chord connecting any two process points P_i and P_j represents all possible production programs which (a) utilize only Process i and j, and (b) yield a total net revenue of $1.

Figure 2 was drawn so that if a chord be drawn between any two non-adjacent process points, then all intermediate process points will lie below it. For example, P_2, P_3, P_4 all lie below the straight line connecting P_1 and P_5. This figure was drawn in this way in order to include only processes which constitute efficient uses of the two scarce resources. For suppose that there were a process which consumed the two fixed factors in a ratio intermediate between Processes 1 and 5 and whose unit level point lay above the chord. Draw the radius vector connecting this point to the origin. Where this radius vector intersects the chord between P_1 and P_5 we have two alternative plans which consume the same amounts of the two fixed factors: first, some combination of Processes 1 and 5 and, second, some level of the intermediate

process. Now the combination of Processes 1 and 5 will yield a
net revenue of $1 while the intermediate process at that level
will yield a net revenue of less than $1 since its unit point lies
beyond the chord. Consequently the intermediate process would be
a less profitable use of the two fixed factors than the equivalent combination of Processes 1 and 5. If, on the other hand,
the unit level of the intermediate process lay below the chord,
then that process would represent a more efficient use of the
fixed resources than the equivalent combination of Process 1 and
5.

This is the geometrical analogue of the simplex criterion
adduced for the general case. Explicitly stated this analogue
is: two processes constitute an efficient basis only if no unit
process points lie below the line connecting the unit points of
the two processes. This statement will be proved below. An
interesting consequence of it is that if a broken line be drawn
through all the points which can enter into efficient bases, as
in figure 2, that line will be convex to the origin. This convexity is obviously strongly analogous to the convexity of a
conventional isoquant. Indeed, this broken line is an isoquant,
for the net revenues resulting from all the production plans
which lie on it are the same, namely $1. Clearly, isoquants for
any other net revenue can be drawn in the same manner, and they
will be similar, in the strict geometrical sense, to the isoquant for $1 net revenue.

We shall now show that the simplex criterion is equivalent
to the statement that two processes constitute an efficient basis only if no process unit points lie below the line connecting
their unit points. Let us consider a basis made up of Processes 1 and 5. If no unit points are to lie below their connecting line we require for all unit process points, $P_i = (a_{i1}, a_{i2})$
that:

if $a_{i1} < a_{51}$,

$$\frac{a_{i2} - a_{52}}{a_{51} - a_{i1}} \geq \frac{a_{12} - a_{52}}{a_{51} - a_{11}} ;$$

if $\qquad a_{i1} > a_{51}$,

$$\frac{a_{52} - a_{i2}}{a_{i1} - a_{51}} \leq \frac{a_{12} - a_{52}}{a_{51} - a_{11}}$$

By clearing of fractions, both of these inequalities can be reduced to:

$$a_{11}a_{i2} - a_{12}a_{i1} + a_{i1}a_{52} - a_{i2}a_{51} \leq a_{11}a_{52} - a_{12}a_{51}.$$

This equation can be written in the form:

$$\begin{vmatrix} a_{11} & a_{i1} \\ a_{12} & a_{i2} \end{vmatrix} + \begin{vmatrix} a_{i1} & a_{51} \\ a_{i2} & a_{52} \end{vmatrix} \leq \begin{vmatrix} a_{11} & a_{51} \\ a_{12} & a_{52} \end{vmatrix}$$

Now the simplex criterion for this case is

$$q_{i1} + q_{i5} \geq 1$$

where q_{i1} and q_{i5} are the solutions to

$$\begin{pmatrix} a_{11} & a_{51} \\ a_{12} & a_{52} \end{pmatrix} \begin{pmatrix} q_{i1} \\ q_{i5} \end{pmatrix} = \begin{pmatrix} a_{i1} \\ a_{i2} \end{pmatrix}$$

Solving for q_{i1} and q_{i5} and substituting in the criterion we obtain:

$$\frac{\begin{vmatrix} a_{i1} & a_{51} \\ a_{i2} & a_{52} \end{vmatrix} + \begin{vmatrix} a_{11} & a_{i1} \\ a_{12} & a_{i2} \end{vmatrix}}{\begin{vmatrix} a_{11} & a_{51} \\ a_{12} & a_{52} \end{vmatrix}} \geq 1$$

Since the denominator of this expression is negative, the criterion derived from the geometry of the two factor case is seen to be identical with the simplex criterion for that case.

A by-product of this analysis is the fact that if a production plan using two processes is to be used, the two processes should be adjacent, that is, there should be no third process available whose radius vector lies between the radius vectors of the

two processes in the basis unless the unit point of this third
process lies above the chord connecting the two unit process points
in the basis. For example, P_1 and P_5 can never form an efficient
basis while P_1 and P_2 can, the reason being that the line connecting P_1 and P_2 lies below the line connecting P_1 and P_5.

In order to maximize its total net return, the firm strives to
get on the highest possible isoquant. This is illustrated in figure 3, which is the same as Figure 2 except that the limitations
on the supplies of the fixed factors are shown. In this figure s_1
represents the total available supply of Factor 1 and s_2 the total
supply of Factor 2 and L represents the point (s_1, s_2). The firm,
then, has the choice of any production schedule represented by a
point inside the rectangle Os_1Ls_2. Point L is the

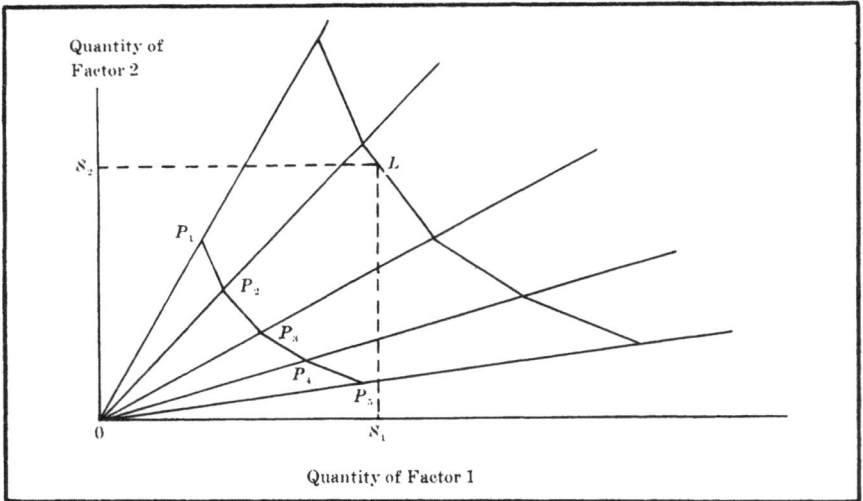

Fig. 3. *Optimum production plan, two factor case.*

point of maximum profits since it lies on the highest possible
isoquant. It should be noted that each segment of the isoquant
through Point L is parallel to the corresponding segment of the
isoquant for $1 net revenue.

Since L which represents a consumption of s_1 units of Factor
1 and s_2 units of Factor 2, lies on the segment of its isoquant
which connects the rays for Processes 2 and 3, the plan it represents can be achieved by an appropriate combination of just
those two processes. Inspection of the figure shows that three
possible cases can arise:

1. L might lie on one or another of the radius vectors. In that case, the process corresponding to that vector should be used up to the point where the supplies of both factors are fully utilized. The production plan would then consist of a single process, used up to the full capacity of the firm;

2. L might lie between two of the radius vectors, as in the case illustrated. In that case, the optimum production plan is a combination of two processes, the two which bracket the supply-limitation point;

3. L might lie outside the pencil of radius vectors. For example, it might lie between the vector through P_1 and the vertical axis. In that case the firm should use Process 1 until the supply of Factor 1 is exhausted and discard the excess supply of Factor 2 by means of a "disposal process."

In no case where there are two factors in limited supply, however, does the optimum production plan require the use of more than two processes.

6. *Price Imputation for Fixed Factors*

Linear programming, like the bulk of formal economic theory, is concerned with the efficient allocation of scarce resources. In economic theory, the determination of price and the allocation of resources are so closely related that they are inseparable topics. This is true also in the linear programming approach. Although we have treated fixed resources thus far as though they had no price, a pricing problem and its solution existed under the surface, as it were. We shall now turn our attention to the price implications of linear programming.

The real cost of the use of any good for any purpose is the alternative opportunities for its use which must be foregone. This is the well established basis for "opportunity cost" or "transfer price." Recognition of this principle is also at the root of linear programming, which rests on an enumeration of all the opportunities available for the application of a given set of resources. Unlike conventional theory, however, linear programming appears to arrive at an optimum allocation without recourse to the concept of price. Actually, as we shall now see, a problem of pricing or valuation is implicit in the linear programming problem and the solution of the latter problem has already, essentially, solved the former.

Let us examine first what is meant by "valuation" in the context of linear programming. It has two aspects: the valuation of the fixed resources of the firm considered as a whole, and the assignment of values to units of individual resources.

Considered as a whole, the value of the firm's fixed assets lies in the fact that they make available a set of production opportunities, and we have already seen how it is possible to select an optimum set from among these opportunities. So far as the resources are of a fixed and enduring nature, the opportunities presented may extend for a considerable period into the future. The questions of discounting future income, with allowance for time preferences and uncertainties are no different from the point of view of linear programming than from that of conventional theory, and they will not be discussed here. All that linear programming has to contribute is a basis for finding the maximum net revenue which these resources can be made to yield during the first time-period, say, the first year. This net revenue may be regarded as the value of the services of the fixed resources for the current time-period.

The second, and more interesting, aspect of the valuation problem is concerned with ascribing values to the services of the several resources separately. (Since the value of a resource is the value of its services discounted to the present time, the shorter phrase will be used throughout the discussion for convenience.) The matter is of practical importance whenever the time-horizon of decisions is great enough to permit adjustments in the holding of durable capital equipment. Which types of resources should be acquired and which disposed of? The question can be answered only by comparing the value of the contribution of each resource to net revenue with its acquisition cost or disposal price. The valuation of resources bears also on the theoretical question of the relationship between the optimum production plan resulting from a linear programming analysis and the allocation of resources which would result from either a free price system or the kind of quasi-pricing system adopted by many firms for purposes of cost accounting.

The value of a capital asset is generally regarded as equivalent to the value of its contribution to the output of the firm. Where several factors coöperate in the production of final products some technique for disentangling their individual contributions is required. This is the purpose of computing the net marginal product in standard treatments, but the marginal concept cannot be applied to a situation where a change in the quantities of an individual factor requires revision of the entire production plan, as is the case where the linear programming model applies. In such cases the value of the contribution of each factor may be deduced from the principle that these values must in total account for the entire net revenue of the firm when the optimum production program is employed.

Consider a firm which has available to it k production processes (including disposal processes) for the employment of n fixed factors. As before, we shall denote these processes by column vectors such as

$$P_i = (a_{i1} \ a_{i2} \ \cdots \ a_{in}), \ i = 1, 2, \ldots, k.$$

We shall use v_i to denote the net revenue yielded by a unit of Process P_i. Of course, v_i will be unity if P_i is an active process and zero if it is a disposal process.

We have already seen that, except in degenerate cases, the optimum program will include just n processes at positive levels. Let the numbering be such that these are the first n processes. We shall denote the matrix composed of the P_i by B so that

$$B = (P_1 \ P_2 \ \cdots \ P_k)$$

and shall partition this matrix into two parts, as follows:

$$B_1 = (P_1 \ P_2 \ \cdots \ P_n),$$

$$B_2 = (P_{n+1} \ P_{n+2} \ \cdots \ P_k).$$

We shall also use the net revenue vectors

$$V_1 = (v_1 \ v_2 \ \cdots \ v_n)$$

$$V_2 = (v_{n+1} \ v_{n+2} \ \cdots \ v_k)$$

$$V = (V_1' \ V_2')',$$

the vectors describing the optimum production plan

$$X_1 = (x_1 \quad x_2 \quad \cdots \quad x_n)$$

$$X_2 = (x_{n+1} \quad x_{n+2} \quad \cdots \quad x_k)$$

$$X = (X_1' \quad X_2')',$$

and the vector of available supplies of fixed factors

$$S = (s_1 \quad s_2 \quad \cdots \quad s_n).$$

All of these are defined to be column vectors; the primes (′) indicating transpositions.

Assume, now, that some value, u_j, is imputed to the services of a unit of the jth fixed factor and define the column vector

$$U = (u_1 \quad u_2 \quad \cdots \quad u_n).$$

Consider Process P_i. We shall define its unit imputed cost to be the sum of the quantities of the fixed factors used at unit level of operation, each multiplied by its imputed value. That is, the unit imputed cost of P_i which we shall denote by t_i, is defined by

$$t_i = a_{i1}u_1 + a_{i2}u_2 + \cdots + a_{in}u_n$$

$$= P_i'U.$$

Since the total net revenue is to be distributed among the fixed factors, if Process P_i is used in the optimum production plan we require

$$t_i = v_i$$

and if Process P_1 is not used we require

$$t_i \geq v_i.$$

These two requirements amount to the condition that no process gives rise to unimputed residual net revenue. The requirement with respect to the n processes in the optimum production plan may be written:

$$B_1'U = V_1.$$

Assuming a non-degenerate case, so that B_1 is not singular, this leads to an explicit expression for the imputed price vector:

$$U = B_1'^{-1} V_1.$$

It remains to be shown that the prices imputed in this way satisfy the requirement for the other processes, successfully distribute the entire maximum net revenue of the firm, and are all positive. Other important properties of this set of prices will also emerge from the discussion.

First we shall show that this set of prices accounts for all the net revenue yielded by each process, that is, that

$$B'U \geq V.$$

This requirement consists, really, of two parts:

$$B_1'U = V_1,$$

$$B_2'U \geq V_2,$$

and U was calculated so as to satisfy the first part. As to the second, let

$$B_2 = B_1 Q,$$

so that the condition becomes

$$Q'B_1'U \geq V_2.$$

Since it was assumed that the processes in B_1 constituted an optimum set, the simplex criterion must be satisfied, that is,

$$Q'V_1 \geq V_2.$$

Now:

$$B_2'U = Q_1'B'U = Q'V_1 \geq V_2$$

since

$$U = B_1'^{-1}V_1.$$

Hence the requirement is satisfied.

It follows at once that none of the elements of U can be negative. For consider the disposal process which corresponds to Factor j. The line of

$$B'U \geq V$$

which corresponds to this process is simply

$$u_j > 0,$$

as desired. It is interesting to note that if any disposal process enters into the optimum plan, the corresponding factor is a free good.

It also follows that this set of imputed prices distributes the maximum net revenue of the firm. This net revenue is, of course,

$$r = V_1' X_1$$

where, as proved previously, X_1 satisfies

$$X_1 = B_1^{-1} S.$$

The total of imputed costs on the basis of this set of imputed prices is $S'U$. We have:

$$S'U = S'B_1'^{-1} V_1 = V_1' B_1^{-1} S = V_1' X_1 = r,$$

as was to be shown.

Now for the moment let us drop the assumption that $B_1' U = V_1$ and let U be any set of imputed prices which distributes the entire net revenue of every process. In other words, we now require only

$$B'U > V.$$

This requires, of course,

$$B_1' U > V_1$$

or

$$B_1' U = V_1 + K_1$$

where K_1 is a vector made up of non-negative elements. The total imputed cost using this set of prices is:

$$\begin{aligned} S'U &= S'(B_1'^{-1} V_1 + B_1'^{-1} K_1) \\ &= V_1' B_1^{-1} S + K_1' B_1^{-1} S \\ &= V_1' X_1 + K_1' X_1 \\ &= r + K_1' X_1 > r. \end{aligned}$$

We have thus shown: If we require that imputed prices distribute the entire net revenue of every available process, then the minimum total imputed cost is just equal to the maximum net revenue, and this minimum is obtained by the set of prices which satisfies

$$B_1'U = V_1.$$

7. *The Concept of the "Dual"*

The problem of valuation may therefore be set up in the following manner: The values to be imputed to the n fixed factors are those such that

$$S'U \text{ is as small as possible,}$$
$$\text{subject to the requirements}$$
$$U \geq 0,$$
$$B'U \geq V.$$

For comparison, we shall rewrite here the problem of finding the optimum production plan. The plan required that the levels of operation of the k processes be such that

$$V'X \text{ is as great as possible,}$$
$$\text{subject to the requirements}$$
$$X \geq 0,$$
$$BX \leq S.$$

These two problems have a strong formal resemblance to each other and both of them depend on the matrix B and the vectors S and V. They are therefore known as "duals" of each other. The phenomenon of the dual seems to have been noticed first in connection with the theory of games and to have been discovered independently by G. W. Brown and J. von Neumann. The mathematical relationships between any linear programming problem and its dual have been studied particularly by Gale, Kuhn, and Tucker (12), and by G. B. Dantzig (7). The leading theorems, both of which were proved above are:

1. The minimum solution of the minimizing member of a dual is exactly equal to the maximum solution of the maximizing member.

If either member of a dual has been solved, the solution of its partner becomes trivial.

The economic significance of duals was first pointed out by P. A. Samuelson in *Market Mechanisms and Maximization* (33) and has been investigated by T. J. Koopmans (19).

We have now seen that the problem of finding an optimal production program and the problem of valuing the fixed factors so as to distribute the total net revenue are duals of each other. The valuation problem can be solved in advance of the programming problem, or the work can be done in reverse order. In some computational procedure, the two problems are solved simultaneously. If either problem is solved, the other becomes trivial.

- - - - - - - - - - - - - - - - - - - -

CHAPTER III

Production Scheduling
for Monopolized Products

1. *The Monopolist's Problem*

In the previous chapter, we considered the production problem facing a firm in perfect competition. The limitation on output and on profit for such a firm is the presence of scarce factors of production and, consequently, the analysis was focused on the maximization of profits within such a limitation. For a monopolist, however, there exists a further limitation. As his output increases the price at which he can dispose of it falls, indicating a progressive saturation of the demand for his output. It has long been known that the presence of a falling demand curve will lead a monopolist to limit his production below the technically feasible limit. (Cournot, 5, p. 56; Marshall, 26, pp. 489 ff.; Robinson, 31, p. 52, to give just a few citations.) We shall now consider this limitation on the output of a monopolist, but our approach will be quite different from that of earlier studies. In particular our approach will emphasize the fact that the monopolist may have only a finite number of productive processes at his disposal. Thus it will be impossible for us (or for him) to perform differentiations with respect to the quantities of the individual productive factors required as inputs. The standard method of analysis, of course, depends quite heavily on the assumption that output is a continuous and differentiable function of each of the inputs. Our analysis will also take account of the fact that the output of each of the available processes may include a number of salable commodities, several of which may be monopolized. Thus, joint production of monopolized commodities will be considered.

Although the analysis will proceed in terms of a firm which produces a number of monopolized products jointly, the principles deduced will have a wider field of application. They apply wherever the marginal utility of output to the producer decreases as quantity increases. They apply, for example, to government monopolies and controlled economies. They apply also to the intermediate products of a large economic enterprise which produces in part for its own use and convenience even if it is not a monopoly.

We shall consider, then, a firm which produces a number of commodities jointly. As before, we shall conceive of this firm as having available a number of distinct processes for producing these products. Each of these processes is characterized by the amount of each commodity produced per dollar spent on the process. So far, the situation is similar to that of the competitive producer discussed previously. But now we shall assume also that the price at which each of the commodities can be marketed depends upon the quantity of that commodity produced by the firm under consideration. It will be assumed also that the firm knows both its production coefficients and its demand curves, and that its objective is to maximize the excess of gross value of sales over direct (variable) costs.

An example of such a firm would be a large silver-mining combine. Silver, nickel, molybdenum, and other metals are found in the same ore and must be extracted together. But different mines will yield these metals in different proportions. The problem facing the combine is to determine how much ore to take out of each of the mines under its control.

We shall deal with the simplest case, where the market price of each commodity is a linear function of the output of that commodity. That is, for the j th commodity we shall assume that

$$P_j = b_j - c_j y_j$$

> where P_j denotes the price of the j th commodity,
>
> y_j denotes the output of the j th commodity,
>
> b_j and c_j are positive constants describing the demand curve for the j th commodity.

The production situation can be described as before by an input-output matrix in which each column shows the quantities of the various products yielded by \$1 spent on a particular process and each row shows for a particular product the quantity of it which will be yielded by \$1 spent on each of the processes in turn. If a_{ij} represents the amount of the jth commodity resulting from spending \$1 on the ith process, x_i represents the expenditure on the ith process, y_j represents the output of the jth commodity, and if the firm has available k processes for producing n products (k greater than n), then the basic production relationships are expressed by the equations:

$$
\begin{pmatrix} y_1 \\ y_2 \\ \cdots \\ y_n \end{pmatrix}
=
\begin{pmatrix} a_{11} & a_{21} & \cdots & a_{k1} \\ a_{12} & a_{22} & & a_{k2} \\ \cdot & \cdot & \cdots & \cdot \\ a_{1n} & a_{2n} & & a_{kn} \end{pmatrix}
\begin{pmatrix} x_1 \\ x_2 \\ \cdots \\ x_k \end{pmatrix}
$$

Allowing capital letters to denote matrices composed of the corresponding small letters, this may be written compactly as:

$$Y = AX$$

The price relationship may also be written as a matrix equation:

$$
\begin{pmatrix} P_1 \\ P_2 \\ \cdots \\ P_n \end{pmatrix}
=
\begin{pmatrix} b_1 - c_1 y_1 \\ b_2 & c_2 y_2 \\ \cdot & \cdots & \cdot \\ b_n & c_n y_n \end{pmatrix}
$$

This matrix equation is equivalent to:

$$
\begin{pmatrix} P_1 \\ P_2 \\ P_3 \\ \cdots \\ P_n \end{pmatrix}
=
\begin{pmatrix} b_1 \\ b_2 \\ b_3 \\ \cdots \\ b_n \end{pmatrix}
-
\begin{pmatrix} c_1 & 0 & 0 & \cdots & 0 \\ 0 & c_2 & 0 & \cdots & 0 \\ 0 & 0 & c_3 & \cdots & 0 \\ \cdot & \cdot & \cdot & \cdots & \cdot \\ 0 & 0 & 0 & \cdots & c_n \end{pmatrix}
\begin{pmatrix} y_1 \\ y_2 \\ y_3 \\ \cdots \\ y_n \end{pmatrix}
$$

Just as before, this can be written compactly as

$$P = B - CY$$

Here it should be noted that P, B, and Y are column matrices, while C is a square matrix with non-zero elements in the diagonal.

We shall denote transposed matrices by primes ($'$) so that, for example, Y' denotes the row of matrix made up of y_1, y_2, $\cdots$, y_n and $1'$ denotes a row of ones (the number of ones in the row will generally be clear). Using this notation, the gross revenue from sales is:

$$g = Y'P$$

and the excess of gross revenue over direct costs is:

$$r = Y'P - 1'X.$$

This is the quantity to be maximized. But first it will be simplified by eliminating the Y-vector from the expression for r. Substituting first for P, we have:

$$r = Y'(B - CY) - 1'X$$

$$= Y'B - Y'CY - 1'X.$$

Now, $Y = AX$ so that $Y' = X'A'$. Also, since $Y'B$ is a one-element matrix, $Y'B = B'Y$. We can now write:

$$r = B'AX - X'A'CAX - 1'X$$

$$= E'X - X'DX$$

$$\text{where } E = A'B - 1$$

$$D = A'CA$$

Net revenue has now been expressed directly as a function of the levels at which the various processes are operated. We note that the first term in this expression is a linear form in x_i, while the second term is a quadratic form.

2. *The Optimum Program*

The standard procedure at this stage of the maximization process would be to differentiate the expression for r with respect to each of the variables x_i and equate the derivatives to zero. Brief consideration will show that this procedure has to be modified in the present instance. In the first place, solution of these equations may lead to negative levels of production, an economically meaningless result. In the second place, whatever the optimum production schedule, it will result in producing various quantities of at most n different commodities. But we have seen previously that the most efficient way to produce stated quantities of n different commodities will involve at most n different production processes. Therefore the solution of the monopolist's problem will involve at most n production processes at positive levels and the rest at zero level. The presence of processes at zero level changes the requirement on the derivatives at the profit-maximizing point. For each process operated at a positive level it remains true that either an increase or a decrease in the level of operation will result in a reduction in profit, so that the derivative of profit with respect to the level of each such process must be zero. But with regard to the processes operated at zero level we need require only that an increase in the level result in a decrease in profit; a decrease in level is physically impossible. Thus with respect to the processes which are not used in the optimum schedule we require only that the derivatives be non-positive. This is, of course, a weaker restriction than the usual one, but it adds the difficulty that we cannot tell in advance which of the processes are not to be used.

Nevertheless, the derivatives of profit with respect to the levels of the available processes will play an important part in the development and will be calculated now. The first term in the expression for r is:

$$E'X = e_1 x_1 + e_2 x_2 + \cdots + e_k x_k,$$

where e_i denotes the ith element of E

So:

$$\frac{d}{dx_i} E'X = e_i.$$

The differentiation of $X'DX$ is accomplished similarly by writing out $X'DX$ explicitly as a quadratic form in x_i and differentiating straightforwardly. This yields:

$$\frac{d}{dx_i} X'DX = 2(d_{i1} \ d_{i2} \ \cdots \ d_{ik})X,$$

where the d_{ij} are the elements of D.

Then, using these two results:

$$\frac{dr}{dx_i} = e_i - 2(d_{i1}\ d_{i2}\ \cdots\ d_{ik})X.$$

If R denote the column vector whose elements are the derivatives just computed,

$$R = E - 2DX.$$

This is the vector of the marginal net revenues of the n processes.

The requirement on an optimum production schedule can now be written formally in terms of this result. It is as follows: A production schedule, X, is optimal only if:

1. $X \geq 0$.

2. $DX \geq \frac{1}{2}E$.

3. The equality sign in Condition 2 holds for all elements corresponding to processes operated at positive levels, the inequality for all elements corresponding to processes operated at zero level.

The first condition merely states the common-sense fact that no process can be operated at a negative level. The second condition states that it must not be profitable to increase the level of operation of any process, that is, that no process has a positive marginal net revenue. The third condition states that the marginal net revenue must be zero for all processes which are operated at a positive level.

An intuitive proof of the necessity of this requirement has already been given. A formal proof will now be presented both in order to establish the condition rigorously and in order to indicate computational procedures for actual numerical problems. The method of proof will be as follows. First we shall select any t processes, $t \leq n$, and denote them as Selection No. 1. Then we shall assume that levels of operation of the remaining $k\text{-}t$ processes have been preassigned. On this assumption we shall compute the optimum levels of the t processes in Selection No. 1, and the resultant maximum profit. Then by setting the levels of all processes not in Selection No. 1 at zero this formula will show the maximum profit, say r^*, which can be obtained by use of those t

processes alone. Further, r^* can be differentiated with respect to each of the processes excluded from Selection No. 1. If any of these derivatives is positive with respect to an excluded process, it will indicate that profits can be increased by including that process in the production program.

Let us suppose, for convenience, that the t processes in Selection No. 1 are the first t in order of number. Then the input-output matrix can be partitioned into two parts, A_1 corresponding to the processes in Selection No. 1, and A_2 corresponding to all the other processes. We have, then:

$$A_1 = \begin{pmatrix} a_{11} & a_{21} & \cdots & a_{t1} \\ a_{12} & a_{22} & \cdots & a_{t2} \\ \cdots\cdots\cdots\cdots\cdots \\ a_{1n} & a_{2n} & \cdots & a_{tn} \end{pmatrix}$$

$$A = \begin{pmatrix} a_{t+1,1} & a_{t+2,1} & \cdots & a_{k1} \\ a_{t+1,2} & a_{t+2,2} & \cdots & a_{k2} \\ \cdots\cdots\cdots\cdots\cdots\cdots \\ a_{t+1,n} & a_{t+2,n} & \cdots & a_{kn} \end{pmatrix}$$

$$A = (A_1 \quad A_2)$$

Then the formula for the output of commodities in terms of the levels of operation is:

$$Y = AX = (A_1 \quad A_2) \begin{pmatrix} X_1 \\ X_2 \end{pmatrix} = A_1 X_1 + A_2 X_2$$

where X_1 is the vector of the levels of operation of the t processes in Selection No. 1 and X_2 is the vector of the $k-t$ excluded processes

Then the price vector is:

$$P = B - CY = B - CA_1 X_1 - CA_2 X_2.$$

Gross revenue is:

$$g = Y'P = (X_1'A_1' + X_2'A_2') (B - CA_1X_1 - CA_2X_2).$$

When this multiplication is carried out, six rather complicated terms result. Simplification is possible, however, by means of the following notations. Let:

$$E_1 = A_1'B - 1$$

$$E_2 = A_2'B - 1$$

so that E_1, E_2 constitute a partition of the basic matrix, E. We note also that:

$$D = A'CA = \begin{pmatrix} A_1' \\ A_2' \end{pmatrix} C (A_1 \ A_2) = \begin{pmatrix} A_1'CA_1 & A_1'CA_2 \\ A_2'CA_1 & A_2'CA_2 \end{pmatrix}$$

Thus D has been split into four sub-matrices. Denote them by D_{11}, D_{12}, D_{21}, D_{22} respectively. We note that, since C is symmetric, $D_{21} = D_{12}'$.

After multiplication and simplification, we obtain in terms of these sub-matrices:

$$g = X_1'(E_1 + 1) - X_1'D_{11}X_1 - 2X_2'D_{21}X_1 + X_2'(E_2 + 1) - X_2'D_{22}X_2$$

From this we obtain at once:

$$r = g - 1'X_1 - 1'X_2$$

$$= E_1'X_1 - 2X_2'D_{21}X_1 - X_1'D_{11}X_1 + E_2'X_2 - X_2'D_{22}X_2.$$

r has now been expressed as a function of X_1 and X_2. For the present we shall regard X_2 as fixed and attempt to maximize r with respect to X_1. Although we could not apply a straightforward maximizing procedure before, we can do so now since X_1 comprises n or fewer processes. Differentiating with respect to the elements of X_1 we obtain, as before,

$$R_1 = E_1 - 2D_{12}X_2 - 2D_{11}X_1.$$

This is the vector of the marginal net revenues of the t processes in Selection No. 1, when the other processes have been pre-assigned the values of the vector X_2. Setting each of these marginal net revenues equal to zero, the value of the optimum X_1 vector is obtained:

$$X_1^* = \tfrac{1}{2}D_{11}^{-1}E_1 - D_{11}^{-1}D_{12}X_2$$

Some of the components of X_1^* may turn out to be negative. Since this can be avoided merely by dropping the appropriate processes from Selection No. 1, thus reducing t, we shall assume that this does not happen, and that $X_1^* > 0$.

To compute the maximum profit, substitute X_1^* for X_1 in the formula for r, obtaining, after simplification:

$$r^* = \tfrac{1}{4}E_1'D_{11}^{-1}E_1 + X_2'(D_{12}'D_{11}^{-1}D_{12} - D_{22})X_2 + (E_2' - E_1'D_{11}^{-1}D_{12})X_2.$$

This is the maximum profit which can be obtained when the k-t levels, X_2, have been preassigned, and

$$r^* = \tfrac{1}{4}E_1' \, D_{11}^{-1}E_1$$

is the maximum profit when $X_2 = 0$. It is now necessary to differentiate r^* with respect to the components of X_2. If any of these derivatives, which are just the net marginal revenues, should be greater than zero when $X_2 = 0$, then the corresponding processes could profitably be introduced into the production plan. The vector of the derivatives is:

$$R^* = (E_2 - D_{12}'D_{11}^{-1}E_1) + 2(D_{12}'D_{11}^{-1}D_{12} - D_{22})X_2.$$

When $X_2 = 0$, only the first term appears. Thus, we have the criterion that Selection No. 1 is optimum if

$$E_2 - D_{12}'D_{11}^{-1}E_1 \leq 0.$$

$$\text{Since } D_{11-}^{-1}E_1 = 2X_1,$$

This is easily seen to be equivalent to the optimality requirement given previously, which is therefore proved. If the criterion is not satisfied, the processes corresponding to the elements for which the inequality goes in the wrong direction should be introduced into the production plan.

The special case for which $t = n$ is of particular importance and permits further simplification. In this case, A_1 is a square matrix which we shall assume to be non-vanishing. We can thus express A_2 as the product of A_1 and a transformation matrix Q, as follows: $A_1Q = A_2$

$$Q = A_1^{-1}A_2.$$

The Q matrix has a clear economic significance which will be discussed as soon as the equations involving it have been deduced.

By use of this Q transformation, the D matrix can be simplified as follows:

$$D = A'CA = \begin{pmatrix} A_1' \\ Q'A_1' \end{pmatrix} C \ (A_1 \ A_1 Q) = \begin{pmatrix} A_1'CA_1 & A_1'CA \ Q_1 \\ Q'A_1'CA_1 & Q'A_1'CA_1 Q \end{pmatrix}$$

$$= \begin{pmatrix} D_{11} & D_{11}Q \\ Q'D_{11} & Q'D_{11}Q \end{pmatrix}$$

And also:

$$E_2 = A_2'B - 1_2 = Q'A_1'B - 1_2 = Q'(E_1 + 1_1) - 1_2$$

$$= Q'E_1 + Q'1_1 - 1_2$$

where 1_1 denotes a column of n ones and 1_2 denotes a column of $k-n$ ones.

When these expressions are inserted in the formula for r^* there results:

$$r^* = \tfrac{1}{4}E_1'D_{11}^{-1}E_1 + X_2'(Q'D_{11}D_{11}^{-1}D_{11}Q - Q'D_{11}Q)X_2 + (E_2' - E_1'Q)X_2.$$

The second term in this expression vanishes and the third can be simplified, yielding, finally:

$$r^* = \tfrac{1}{4}E_1'D_{11}^{-1}E_1 + (1_1'Q - 1_2')X_2.$$

It should be reëmphasized that the test of optimality takes this simple form only when the selection being tested includes exactly n processes, all operated at positive levels. In that case, the test is as follows: add the elements in each column of Q and subtract unity from the sum. If the result of this computation is zero or negative for every column of Q, the selection being tested is optimal and the maximum obtainable profit is $\tfrac{1}{4}E_1'D_{11}^{-1}E_1$. If the result of the computation is positive for any column or columns then the selection being tested is not optimal and profit can be increased by adding to the schedule the processes corresponding to the positive columns. Since it is known that the optimum production schedule cannot include more than n

processes (one for each salable commodity), this necessarily involves dropping some of the processes included in the selection being tested. The details of this calculation will be given below. For the present we shall turn to the economic significance of the Q matrix.

The meaning of the Q-matrix can best be appreciated by examining a typical column, say the column denoted by the subscript j, $n \leq j \leq k$. This column is computed from the equation:

$$\begin{pmatrix} a_{11} & a_{21} & \cdots & a_{n1} \\ a_{12} & a_{22} & \cdots & a_{n2} \\ \cdot & \cdot & \cdots & \cdot \\ a_{1n} & a_{2n} & \cdots & a_{nn} \end{pmatrix} \begin{pmatrix} q_{j1} \\ q_{j2} \\ \cdots \\ q_{jn} \end{pmatrix} = \begin{pmatrix} a_{j1} \\ a_{j2} \\ \cdots \\ a_{jn} \end{pmatrix}$$

This means that if the firm spent q_{j1} dollars on the first process, q_{j2} dollars on the second process, and so on up to q_{jn} dollars on the nth process the resulting output of all commodities would be the same as if it had spent \$1 on the jth process. Thus this column amounts to the specification of the combination of the first n processes which is equivalent to the jth. If, then,

$$q_{j1} + q_{j2} + \cdots + q_{jn} < 1$$

the jth process is less economical than the equivalent combination of the first n processes, while if the inequality goes in the opposite direction the jth process is more economical than the equivalent combination. The test of the optimality of r^* is precisely the computation of these k-n inequalities.

We are now in a position to propose a procedure for the practical computation of an optimum production schedule. The procedure will consist of starting with any promising production schedule, testing it, and then gradually modifying it by means of an iterative process until a schedule which satisfies the optimizing requirement is found.

The first step is to decide on any promising selection of n processes. This can be done as follows: consider each of the k available processes in turn and compute the maximum profit which can be earned by utilizing that process alone. Then select as a starting point for the iterative procedure the n

processes which have the greatest maximum individual profits. This criterion has the virtue of eliminating from consideration all processes which are money-losers or nearly so.

In order to compute the maximum profit obtainable from a production schedule consisting of a single process, say the ith, apply the formula for r^* with Selection No. 1 consisting of the ith process alone and $X_2 = 0$ Then the matrices reduce to single elements $(e.g., D_{11} = D_{ii})$ and we find for the maximum profit obtainable by use of process i alone,

$$r^* = \frac{1}{4} \frac{e_i^2}{d_{ii}}$$

This is an easy computation, once the D and E matrices have been calculated. The n processes which lead to the largest values of r^*, considered individually, will constitute Selection No. 1.

The next step is to calculate the optimum levels of the n processes in Selection No. 1 when they are operated jointly. The formula for this has already been found. It is:

$$X_1^* = \frac{1}{2} D_{11}^{-1} E_1.$$

Two cases can now arise: Either all the components of X_1^* are positive or some of them are zero or negative. Case No. 1, where all components are positive, will be considered first. In this case, Selection No. 1 constitutes a selection of n processes, all operated at a positive level. Therefore the simpler test for optimality applies. The test consists in computing the Q matrix and finding the sum of the elements in each of its columns. If all of these sums are less than unity, Selection No. 1 is optimal and the problem has been solved. If any of these sums exceed unity, select the process corresponding to the largest sum. This process is to be added to the program to the largest extent possible. Say it is the jth. The limitation on the level of the jth process arises from the fact that as the level of this process is increased, the levels of some of the first n processes decrease until finally one of them is wiped out. In fact, if X_2 is made up of zeros except for a x_j in its $(j-n)$ th element the formula for X_1^* becomes:

$$X_{11}^* = \frac{1}{2} D_{11}^{-1} E_1 - x_j (q_{j1} \ q_{j2} \ \cdots \ q_{jn})'$$

since $D_{11}^{-1}D_{12} = Q.$

The process which will be wiped out first is the one for which the ratio of the corresponding element of $D_{11}^{-1}E_1$ to the corresponding q_{ji} is smallest. Say it is the ith process. Then the original schedule of processes can be improved by dropping the ith process and adding the jth. This new schedule can be tested in the same way, and the procedure iterated until a basis is found with respect to which no excluded process is economical. Profits will be increased at each stage of the iteration and, when it concludes, will be at the maximum possible level.

In Case No. 2, some of the components of X_1^* turn out to be negative. The economic significance of such a result is that it is not profitable to use the processes corresponding to the negative components in conjunction with the processes corresponding to the positive components. All the processes which correspond to negative components should, therefore, be dropped from the production program. This leaves an initial selection in which there are fewer than n processes, that is, fewer processes than products. Application of the basic optimality criterion will indicate which processes, if any, can be added to this program profitably. Processes can, of course, be added without forcing any to be dropped until a maximum of n processes is obtained. The proximate objective in adding processes in this case should be to obtain a production program which includes exactly n processes, all at positive levels. When such a program has been obtained, we are in the situation of Case No. 1, and the calculation of the optimum can proceed readily. The procedure can terminate, of course, before a n process program has been obtained if, at any stage, it turns out that there are no processes with respect to which the first derivatives of r^* are positive. In this event, the optimum production program has been found, even though it includes fewer processes than products.

3. *Application to Monopsony*

This same technique may be applied to the analysis of a firm in perfect competition which experiences rising costs of production. Increases in production cost may take either of two forms. First, as output increases the firm may be compelled by exhaustion of fixed resources to resort to more expensive production processes. This type of cost increase was dealt with in detail in chapter ii. Second, as production increases the firm may find it necessary to pay higher prices for the resources it purchases from the outside. It is to this type of cost increase—the monopsonistic type—that we now turn our attention.

Suppose that a firm purchases n different resources under monopsonistic conditions. We shall assume that the supply curves for these resources are linear, so that the price of the ith resource can be expressed as:

$$P_i = b_i + c_i y_i,$$

$$i = 1, 2, \ldots, n,$$

where y_i denotes the quantity purchased.

Then, just as in the monopoly case, the price vector can be written:

$$P = B + CY$$

The definitions of P, B, C, and Y are exactly the ones used before, except that Y is now a vector of inputs rather than of outputs. We assume, as before, that the firm has k processes available, denoted by:

$$P_j = (a_{j1} \ a_{j2} \ \cdots \ a_{jn})',$$

$$J = 1, 2, \ldots, k.$$

This notation states that if process P_j is used at a level which will yield a gross revenue of \$1, it will consume a_{ji} units of the ith resource. This mode of definition implies, of course, that the firm's outputs are sold under conditions of pure competition.

Let:
$$A = (P_1 \ P_2 \ \cdots \ P_k),$$

a k-column, n-row matrix, and let

$$X = (x_1 \ x_2 \ \cdots \ x_k)'$$

be the intensity vector for the k processes. Then

$$Y = AX$$

expresses the consumption of inputs in terms of the process intensities and

$$P = B + CAX$$

expresses the price vector in terms of the process intensities. Gross revenue is given by

$$\text{Gross revenue} \quad 1'X$$

and total direct expenses by

$$\text{Direct costs} = P'Y$$

$$= (B' + X'A'C)AX$$

$$= B'AX + X'A'CAX.$$

Net revenue, the excess of gross revenue over direct costs, is

$$r = (1' - B'A)X - X'A'CAX.$$

The problem is to maximize this function subject to the requirement $X \leq 0$.

If this formulation is now compared with the revenue function encountered in the analysis of the monopolist's problem, it will be seen that the two are identical except for the sign of the linear term. We do not need to repeat the analysis, therefore, but merely point out that the procedure and conclusions developed in the monopolistic case apply without modification to the monopsonistic case as well.

4. *Quadratic Programming*

In the first two sections of this chapter we arrived at what amounted to a valuation of monopoly opportunity. We there posed the problem of the monopolistic firm which had sufficient resources to take full advantage of its market position and derived a formula for the maximum profit obtainable from such monopoly power. In practice, of course, the monopolist will frequently not be able to enjoy the full monopoly profit derived from this formula, for a variety of reasons. And one of these reasons is that before he has exploited his monopoly position to the full he will find himself limited by his productive capacity, at least in the short run. A large element of unreality can be removed from our analysis by taking account of the limitations of fixed plant and equipment, and we turn now to the study of the monopolistic firm subject of resource limitations. Just as this problem is a combination of the two problems we have already dealt with, so the technique of analysis will be a combination of the techniques used in chapter ii and in the earlier sections of this chapter.

As before, we conceive of the monopolist as having access to k productive processes, a unit of each productive process being defined as that level of operation which requires \$1 in direct expenses. These k processes involve among them the consumption of m factors of production whose availability to the firm is subject to an absolute limitation. To describe this we introduce the following notation:

h_{ij} = the number of units of the ith limited factor consumed by one unit of the jth production process;

z_i = the total consumption of the ith limited factor;

s_i = the available supply of the ith limited factor;

x_j = the level of operation of the jth process, just as in previous sections.

Then the quantities of limited factors consumed are given by:

$$
\begin{pmatrix} z_1 \\ z_2 \\ \cdots \\ z_m \end{pmatrix} = \begin{pmatrix} h_{11} & h_{12} & \cdots & h_{1k} \\ h_{21} & h_{22} & \cdots & h_{2k} \\ \cdots & \cdots & & \cdots \\ h_{m1} & h_{m2} & & h_{mk} \end{pmatrix} \begin{pmatrix} x_1 \\ x_2 \\ \cdots \\ x_k \end{pmatrix}
$$

or, using compact notation:

$$Z = HX.$$

The limitation imposed by fixed resources may be expressed by writing $S = (s_1 \ s_2 \ \cdots \ s_m)$, a column vector. Then the monopolist strives to maximize his net revenue, $r(X)$ in our previous notation, subject to the limitations

$$Z = HX \leqslant S, \ X \geqslant 0,$$

that is, subject to the limitation that he consumes no more than the available amount of any resource. We recall that

$$r(X) = E'X - X'DX,$$

using the notation and development of section 1.

The problem of the monopolist with fixed resources is thus seen to be an important and fundamental extension of the problem of linear programming. The limitations within which the monopolist must work are the same as those of the competitor of chapter ii, but the function which he wishes to maximize is a quadratic rather than a linear function of the process levels. For this reason we refer to this problem as *quadratic programming*.

Quadratic programming is a significant extension of the range of problems amenable to programming analysis but does not add any new concepts which require exploration. Three questions, however, demand treatment. First, are there any theorems analogous to those found in the linear (competitive) case concerning the number of processes which need be used in order to obtain maximum profit? Second, does the price quantity dualism found in the linear case carry over to the quadratic case? Third, does quadratic programming lead to a theory of monopoly which is consistent with the received theory as derived from marginal utility analysis? To these questions we now turn.

It will be recalled from chapter ii that the decisive step in the solution of linear programming problems was the discovery of theorems which allowed us to state in advance how many different processes had to be used in order to maximize profit. This enabled us to select from the infinitude of possible programs a finite number which included an optimum program. Then we developed a systematic method for picking out an optimum program from among the finite number of possibilities which had to be considered. Now we attack the quadratic programming problem in the same spirit, although it will be too much to expect that the solution will be as convenient as it was in the linear case.

There are two fundamentally different situations with respect to resource limitations which might arise. The first situation is that in which the monopolist obtains his maximum profit without using his total supply of any resource. This situation, in which the resource limitations are ineffective, is the one which we have already dealt with extensively, and nothing more need be said about it. The second situation is that in which the maximizing solution arrived at in the first two sections of this chapter requires more units of at least one resource than is available to the firm. This is the situation which we now discuss.

Two things are clear at once about cases where resource limitations are effective. First, the maximum profit obtainable will be smaller than if there were no effective resource limitations. Second, the optimum production plan will use the full available supply of at least one resource. We shall denote by m_1 the number of resources whose complete supplies are utilized by an optimum program, and will assume that $1 \leqslant m_1 \leqslant m$. We shall similarly denote by k_1, $1 \leqslant k_1 \leqslant k$, the number of productive processes used at positive levels in the optimum production plan. Following the method of linear programming we search for a relationship between m_1 and k_1.

It will be convenient to make the same non-degeneracy assumptions which in the linear case avoided mathematical difficulties without incurring serious practical limitations on the results. We therefore assume that the columns of H are linearly independent, that is, that it is impossible to express any column of H as a linear function of $m-1$ or fewer other columns. Economically this means that no combination of $m-1$ or fewer productive processes can be found which will consume precisely the same quantities of each limited resource as some process not in the combination. We also assume that the supply vector, S, is linearly independent of every set of less than m columns of H, that is, that at least m productive processes must be used in order to use up the available supplies of all m factors. We also make a stricter assumption. In an optimum program subject to resource limitations a certain number, m_1, of the resources will be completely exhausted. That is, m_1 of the elements of Z will be equal to the corresponding elements of S. We assume that this is impossible unless at least m_1 processes are used, that is, unless $k_1 \geqslant m_1$. In algebraic terms we may think of taking any sub-set of m_1 elements of S and the corresponding m_1 rows of H. Denote these two sub-sets by S_1 and H_1 respectively. Then we have assumed that S_1 is linearly independent of any selection of less than m_1 columns of H_1. Economically, we have assumed that it is impossible to exhaust the supplies of m_1 limited resources by any combination of less than m_1 processes.

These assumptions provide a lower limit for k_1:

$$m_1 \leqslant k_1.$$

It can be shown that the upper limit is given by $n+m_1$, where n is the number of monopolized products. Thus we have the theorem:

$$m_1 \leqslant k_1 \leqslant n+m_1.$$

This theorem is proved by the method employed in deriving the analogous theorem for linear programming in chapter ii, section 2, and need not be repeated in full. The method of proof consists in assuming that an optimum production plan exists for which $k_1 > n+m_1$ If this is so, the levels of the first $n+m_1$ processes used can be expressed as a linear function of the levels of the remaining k_1-n-m_1 processes. Then the levels of these last k_1-n-m_1 processes can be varied at will and corresponding variations in the first $n+m_1$ processes can be found such that net revenue does not change. This makes it possible to find a set of variations such that at least one of the processes is reduced to zero level or, alternatively, such that the number of completely utilized factors has been increased. In either case the excess of k_1 over $n+m_1$ will be reduced. This procedure can be used so long as the number of processes used is greater than $n+m_1$. Thus if an optimum production plan exists for which the number of processes used exceeds the number of products plus the number of effectively scarce resources, then there is also a plan which affords the same net revenue and for which the number of processes used is no greater than the number of products plus the number of effectively scarce resources. The details of the proof follow closely the partitioning method used in chapter ii, section 2.

We can even make a somewhat stronger statement. Suppose that an optimum program exists for which $k_1 > n+m_1$. Then for any of the k_1 processes used we could find an equivalent combination of $n+m_1$ other processes such that the equivalent combination would consume the same quantities of all limited resources and yield the same quantities of monopolized products per dollar of direct costs as the process itself. Only in the case where such an equivalent combination exists (call it an equi-cost equivalent combination) is it possible for a plan for which $k_1 < n+m_1$ to be an optimum plan. Thus, if equi-cost equivalent combinations exist, there exists an optimum production plan for which $k_1 > n+m_1$; if equi-cost combinations do not exist, and they are unlikely, then only a plan for which $k_1 \leqslant n+m_1$ can be optimal.

This is our desired extension of the basic theorem of linear programming. Formally the extension is an exact analog of the original. But for purposes of application it is much less useful because in the linear case we knew the critical number, n, in advance while in the quadratic (monopolistic) case we do not know m_1 a priori. At any rate we can say in advance that $k \leqslant n+m$ where, it will be remembered, m denotes the total number of fixed resources. It is possible, of course, that a more conclusive result might be obtained by using the device of disposal processes, just as in the competitive case.

The second problem to be explored is the imputation of values to the limited resources in the monopolistic case along the lines which proved so fruitful in the competitive case. Kuhn and Tucker (46) have shown that if an optimum program exists then to it there corresponds a set of numbers which fulfill the mathematical requirements of accounting prices for the scarce resources. We shall make use of their theorem and then go beyond it to show how such accounting prices can be computed in the quadratic programming case.

The prices in question are the values per unit to be assigned to the resources in fixed supply. Such values are useful in internal cost-accounting and as a guide to the future acquisition of plant and capital equipment. We think now of imputing a certain value, to be denoted by u_i, to each unit of the i th fixed factor and define the vector of these imputed values:

$$U = (u_1 \ u_2 \ \dots \ u_m).$$

Corresponding to any value vector, U, there is an accounting cost for each of the k processes. Since each process has been defined so as to consume fixed factors in constant proportions and, moreover, requires \$1 per unit in direct costs to operate, there is no distinction between marginal and average costs for a process. Let us denote the unit accounting cost of the j th process by t_j. We have:

$$t_j = h_{1j}u_1 + h_{2j}u_2 + \ldots + h_m u_m.$$

If T denote $(t_1 \ t_2 \ \ldots \ t_k)$, the vector of accounting costs of all k processes, the last formula may be summarized:

$$T = H'U.$$

It should be noted that this concept of accounting costs is net of direct dollar costs, just as our concept of net revenue is, and measures exclusively the consumption of limited resources.

The foregoing indicates how the accounting costs, once assigned, enter our formulas. Now it is necessary to assign accounting values to each limited resource and accounting costs to each process and, as a preliminary step, to formulate the characteristics which a useful set of accounting values should possess. In the first place it is clear that they should be non-negative. For if the accounting value of any resource were negative then the imputed costs of all processes which use that resource would be reduced in proportion to the amount of the negative-valued resource which they consumed. Second, the values of resources whose supply is not fully required for an optimum production plan should be zero. In other words, no cost should be charged against any process for using resources for which there is no profitable alternative use. Such resources are free goods from the point of view of the enterprise. Third, each resource should be assigned a value equal to the increase in net revenue which would be obtained if one more unit of the resource were available, or, alternatively, equal to the decrease in net revenue which would be suffered if one less unit were available. That is, the value assigned to each resource should equal the marginal net product it contributes to the production plan as a whole. This requirement is clearly consistent with the first two, but is more specific.

Let us denote the marginal net revenue of the jth process by

$MR(j)$. In section 2 we found

$$MR(j) = e_j - 2D_j'X$$

where $D_j' = (d_{j1}\ d_{j2}\ \cdots\ d_{jk})$, the row vector corresponding to the jth row of D. The marginal cost of the jth process has already been found to be t_j.

Kuhn and Tucker proved in the reference cited that if X denotes an optimum production plan there exists a non-negative vector U such that if t_j is computed according to $T = H'U$, then

$$e_j - 2D_j'X \leqslant t_j.$$

That is, the marginal revenue of each process is no greater than its marginal cost. Furthermore, they showed:

$$(e_j - 2D_j'X)x_j = t_j x_j.$$

This requires that if the marginal revenue of the jth process is less than its marginal cost, then $x_j = 0$. That is, no process is used in an optimum production plan if its marginal revenue is less than its marginal cost. And, conversely, if the jth process is used, so that $x_j > 0$, then marginal revenue and marginal cost must be equal. This theorem establishes the consistency between the quadratic programming approach to the problem of monopoly and the marginal productivity analysis.

These results lead immediately to the theorem that the elements of U which satisfy the Kuhn and Tucker theorem equal the marginal productivities of the m scarce resources. We need only to derive expressions for the marginal productivities of the scarce resources. To do this we consider the marginal value products of the k_1 processes which are used at positive levels in an optimum program. They are:

$$MR(j) = e_j - 2D_j'X, \qquad j = 1, 2, \ldots, k_1.$$

By Kuhn and Tucker's theorem,

$$MR(j) = t_j.$$

Now think of varying the levels x_1, x_2, $\ldots$, x_{k1} by small amounts Δx_1, Δx_2, $\ldots$, Δx_{k_1} respectively. The effect on net revenue will be

$$\Delta r(X) = \sum_{j=1}^{k_1} MR(j) \, \Delta x_j = \sum_{j=1}^{k_1} t_j \, \Delta x_j.$$

Let us choose these variations in such a way that the consumption of the first scarce resource is decreased by one unit while the consumption levels of the other m_1-1 resources in effectively scarce supply are not changed. Then $\Delta r(X)$ is the negative of the marginal productivity of the first scarce resource. We now want to show that $\Delta r(X) = u_1$. Let T_1 denote the cost-vector of k_1 processes used at positive levels and ΔX_1 denote the vector of variations. Then

$$\Delta r(X) = T_1' \, \Delta X_1.$$

Let H_1 denote the first k_1 columns of H. Then

$$T_1 = H_1' U$$

Let ΔZ denote the vector of changes in resource consumption resulting from the changes in process levels ΔX_1. Then

$$\Delta Z = H_1 \, \Delta X_1.$$

But we have selected ΔX_1 so that

$$\Delta Z = (-1 \ 0 \ 0 \ \ldots \ 0)$$

We now substitute in the formula for $\Delta r(X)$:

$$\Delta r(X) = T_1' \, \Delta X_1 = U'H_1 \, \Delta X_1$$

$$= U' \, \Delta Z$$

$$= -u_1,$$

which was to be proved. In order to minimize algebraic detail we have not raised the question of whether a set of variations ΔX_1 can be found which fulfills our assumptions. But it is not difficult to see that such a set of variations can always be found if the number of processes used is at least as great as the number of resources in effectively scarce supply, that is, if $k_1 \geqslant m_1$. And this, according to our basic non-degeneracy assumptions, will always be true.

It is worth noting that u_1 found as we have just found it cannot be negative for, since we began with an optimum set of X, $\Delta r(X)$ cannot be positive. To recapitulate, the rule for finding U is that u_i should be equal to the marginal productivity of the ith limited factor if the supply of that factor is completely exhausted by an optimum plan, and should be equal to zero if the optimum plan does not use the entire supply of the factor. Kuhn and Tucker's theorem shows that such a U composed of non-negative elements always exists if an optimum program exists.

It may be remarked without proof that if

E_1 denotes the first k_1 elements of E,

X_1 denotes the levels of the k_1 processes used at positive levels,

H_{11} denotes the first m_1 rows and k_1 columns of H,

D_{11} denotes the first k_1 rows and columns of D,

T_1 denotes the accounting costs of the k_1 processes included in X_1, and

U_1 denotes the accounting prices of the m_1 limited resources of U which are fully utilized,

then

$$E_1 - 2D_{11}X_1 = T_1 = H'_{11}U_1.$$

By further partitioning, an explicit formula for U_1 can be found from this equation.

As might be expected this set of values lacks one property which we found for the accounting values in the competitive case: it does not exhaust the product. To show this we must show

$$r(X) > U'S,$$

that is, total net revenue exceeds the total imputed value of the limited resources. Now

$$U'(S - Z) = 0$$

because if $s_i - z_i \geqslant 0$ then $u_i = 0$, that is, if there is a surplus of any factor its imputed value is zero. Therefore:

$$U'S = U'Z = U'HX - T'X.$$

We found, further, in our discussion of Kuhn and Tucker's theorem that

$$T'X = E'X - 2X'DX.$$

Thus, writing out the equation for $r(X)$, what we have to show is

$$E'X - X'DX > E'X - 2X'DX,$$

or
$$X'DX > 0.$$

But, referring back to sections 1 and 2, we see that this must be true for a monopolist because

$$X'DX = X'A'CAX = Y'CY.$$

But $Y'CY > 0$ because total gross revenue is

$$Y'P = Y'B - Y'CY$$

and this must be less than the revenue which would be obtained if the monopolists' selling prices did not decrease in response to increases in output. That is:

$$Y'P < Y'B$$

or
$$Y'B - Y'CY < Y'B,$$

or
$$Y'CY > 0.$$

It remains only to notice that the price-quantity duality theorem of linear programming carries over in atrophied form. What remains of it is $U'(S - Z) = 0$, so that U has the property of minimizing the imputed value of the factor surpluses.

We have now set forth the fundamentals of a theory by which the operations of a non-competitive enterprise can be analyzed in programming terms. The advantages of programming analysis, discussed in chapters iii and iv, are just as applicable to non-competitive as to competitive firms, so that the methods of quadratic programming open a fresh range of applications to the programming approach. Non-competitive situations occur frequently in economic analysis. In addition to the monopolists' problem, there is obviously an analogous problem in the field of monopsony. A more important application lies in the field of economic planning. If the S-vector be regarded as the inventory of resources available to a community, the X-vector as the levels of operation of the community's various industries, the H-matrix the community's input matrix, the A-matrix the community's output matrix, and the P-vector a vector of social preferences as a function of the quantities of final output, then the problem of economic planning becomes identical with the monopolist's problem here discussed. Nor need the phrase "economic planning" as here used be restricted to the global operations of a planned economy. The concepts and methods here developed can be applied just as fruitfully to the segmental planning of a mobilization program or to the establishment of norms for the guidance of a free enterprise economy.

- -

CHAPTER IV

Assumptions, Limitations, and Possibilities

In the foregoing chapters we have set forth the basic principles of linear programming and shown how they can be applied to a variety of economic problems. We have seen that the approach is quite flexible. It can deal with pure competition on the one hand and with monopoly and monopsony on the other. It can deal with static problems and with dynamic ones. Although it appears on the surface to make rigid technical assumptions, a flexible technology with scope for complementarity and substitutability are of its very essence. The time has now come to appraise these variations of the linear programming approach, to search out the core which binds them into a single method, and to inquire into the place of that method in economics.

1. *General Postulates of Maximization*

Linear programming is clearly closely related to the marginal analysis because both modes of analysis depend on formal, mathematical methods of maximization. Samuelson (32) has made a very suggestive attempt to show that the formal essence of equilibrium economics can be derived by application of a handful of theorems in the calculus of maxima and minima. His treatment was in terms of the marginal analysis; the logic applies equally to optima derived by means of linear programming.

Both of these methods of analysis, consequently, rest on the postulates of mathematical optimization. So far as they purport to describe economic actions they both postulate that economic decisions are made on the basis of rational calculation. Further, to bring the problem within the scope of mathematics, they both postulate that the guiding objective of economic decisions is to maximize some measurable function of the variables under the control of the decision unit. Although both of these postulates have a strong appeal — what other basis of decision can there be? — both are also open to vigorous criticism. The assumption of rationality implies the existence of the "economic man," an assumption which has been called into increasing question by studies in psychology, business sociology, and institutional economics. The assumption of some formal kind of maximization demands an inordinate amount of information about supply, demand, and the physical conditions of production. The assumption that the quantity to be maximized is measurable slurs over the wealth of inchoate psychic considerations which influence every economic decision.

It appears that no mathematical model simple enough to be manageable can reflect adequately the intricate, blundering decision-making process of the real economic world. Yet simplified models serve a real purpose in enabling us to deal intellectually with at least some of the forces at work in the real economic world. They perform, partly, the function of an experiment under controlled laboratory conditions.

In linear programming to a greater extent than in the marginal analysis there is a conscious attempt to state the economic problem in an operationally meaningful way, that is, to work with concepts which correspond to measurable phenomena and to state the problems in terms of the variables with which businessmen and other economic policy-makers actually operate. The process, with its constant unit direct costs, is a familiar concept to the businessman and his accounting methods are based on this concept (Noyes, 28). By paralleling practical modes of thought, linear programming partly avoids the charge of unreality which has been levelled against the marginal analysis. Indeed, the technique promises to be of considerable value in the field of scientific management. But it shares with older types of formal economic analysis the necessity for restricting itself to rationally controlled decisions and decisions with measurable consequences.

2. The Specific Postulates of Linear Programming

In addition to sharing the assumptions of formal maximization, linear programming invokes four special postulates of its own. These are:

a. Linearity. By definition, in linear programming, each process is characterized by certain ratios of the quantities of the inputs to each other and to the quantities of each of the outputs. These ratios are defined to be constant and independent of the extent to which the process is used.

b. Divisibility. It is assumed that any process can be used to any positive extent so long as sufficient resources are available; indivisibilities and "lumpiness" in production are ignored.

c. Additivity. It is assumed that two or more processes can be used simultaneously, within the limitations of available resources, and that if this is done the quantities of the outputs and inputs will be the sums of the quantities which would result if the several processes were used individually.

d. Finiteness. It is assumed that the number of processes available is finite.

These four assumptions are essential to the mathematical analysis of linear programming problems. We must now inquire into the extent to which they limit the application of linear programming to practical economic questions.

On the surface, at least, the most objectionable of the four assumptions is the first. Yet a moment's thought will show that the linearity assumption of linear programming is quite consistent with the formulation of economic problems made familiar by the marginal analysis. It is a truism of economic analysis that the familiar curvature of production functions is generated by changes in the proportions of the various inputs and not by mere changes in scale. As Knight puts it:

> If the amounts of *all* elements in a combination
> were freely variable without limit and the prod-
> uct also continuously divisible, it is evident
> that one size of combination would be precisely
> similar in its workings to any other similarly
> composed.   (18; p. 98.)

Thus the curvature of production functions is attributable to shifts from one process to another, rather than to changes in the scale of application of any one process.

What, now, would be the shape of a production function which

satisfied the postulate of linearity in this sense? Any point on
a production function is a specification of a set of mutually com-
patible inputs and outputs. The postulate under examination
merely asserts that if we start with any point on the production
function and multiply (or divide) each of the inputs and outputs
by the same positive quantity the resultant point will also lie
on the production function. But this characteristic is nothing
more than the definition of a homogeneous function of the first
order. Consequently, the real force of the linearity postulate is
the familiar assumption that physical production functions are
homogeneous of order one.

The homogeneity of production functions has been the subject of
much economic speculation. F.H. Knight, in the passage quoted above,
treats it as self-evident and T.J. Koopmans has repeatedly invoked an
equivalent axiom which states that so long as resources are available
any production facility can be duplicated exactly, and, if this is
done, each replication will be exactly as productive as the original
facility. Samuelson (32; p.84) has pointed out that the issue is one
of standpoint rather than of fact, analogous, perhaps, to the astrono-
mical question of whether the planets move in epicycles around the
earth or ellipses around the sun. It is sufficient to remark that the
inputs and outputs of a productive process can be defined in such
a way that the production functions are homogeneous and that it is
convenient for many purposes to do this. Linear programming, as
expounded in this essay, takes this standpoint.

Before concluding the discussion of the linearity assumption, it
is important to note that this assumption serves two purposes in
linear programming. The first is a conceptual purpose; it permits
the definition of processes by means of their constant input-output
ratios. The second is a computational convenience; it facilitates
the solution of linear programming problems by the use of systems of
linear inequalities. In some treatments of linear programming (e.g.,
Wood and Geisler, 43), processes have been defined in an intuitive manner and non-linear processes have been introduced. Computational
methods have been devised for dealing with non-linear processes to a
limited extent and Wood and Geisler have asserted that linearity is not
essential to the method. It appears to the present author, however,
that the linearity assumption is not unduly restrictive and that
little is to be gained by abondoning it for most applications.

The divisibility assumption, also, is not seriously restrictive except where the product of an enterprise or economy consists of a few

indivisible items as, for example, in shipbuilding. The inputs involved in any process are of three types: producers' non-durable goods entirely consumed in the process, services of individuals and outside firms, and services of capital equipment owned by the firm in question. The consumption of all these inputs by any process may be varied at will without encountering gross indivisibilities. Thus production processes may be carried out, as assumed, at any desired positive level except in a few rare instances where the output is a significantly discrete variable. For such exceptional instances the range of choice is likely to be so limited that the optimum level of production can be determined merely by enumeration.

The additivity assumption is closely allied to the assumption of linearity. The linearity assumption states that if two or more identical processes are carried on simultaneously the physical results will be additive. The additivity assumption extends this postulate to the case where the processes are not identical. The defense (in a plausibility sense) of this assumption is similar to the defense of the linearity assumption.

It is easy to find instances in which the additivity assumption is apparently violated. In the steel industry, for example, it has been found advantageous to carry on the successive steps from the reduction of ore to the rolling of steel in an integrated fashion in order to save the expense of reheating. This, however, should not be regarded as carrying on a number of separate processes simultaneously but rather as the introduction of a new and more efficient process. The additivity assumption, of course, does not assert that it is efficient to tack a number of distinct processes onto one another, but only that it is possible to do so. This assumption, like that of linearity, is a statement of conceptual formulation rather than one of fact, and it appears to be a useful way to formulate the relationships between processes.

The finiteness assumption is, in reality, the most limiting of the four. In many industries the range of alternatives is effectively infinite. Agriculture is the most important example, but this is equally true of oil refining and the chemical industries in general. In all such industries, the ratios of the inputs and outputs are infinitesimally variable at the will of the management. But there are many other industries where, in the short run at least, only a finite number of productive processes are available (see Lester, 24; p. 72) and even where the range of choice is infinite, the situation may be

approximated to any desired degree of refinement by use of a large
though finite number of discrete processes. Koopmans has pointed
out how this can be done in a number of papers (notably 21; p. 5).

This limitation is not, in reality, either adventitious or even
unfortunate but is of the essence of the point of view adopted by
linear programming. The marginal analysis and linear programming
are both formal simplifications of the production problem. In
order to achieve simplification the two methods seize on different
aspects of the problem as the essential one, and to this extent
they are solutions of different problems. The distinction between
the two methods will be clarified if we examine again the nature of
the productive decisions made by an entrepreneur. We may think of
him as having certain productive resources at his disposal and as
having access to still other resources through the open market.
The resources under his control plus, perhaps, any financial restrictions on his access to the open market define and delimit his
production opportunities. With regard to each of his disposable
resources he has, essentially, two sorts of decisions to make:
first, the use, if any, which he is to make of that resource,
and, second, the technique to be applied for using that resource
for the purpose adopted. Agriculture provides an excellent example for distinguishing these two sorts of decision. Land is
normally the limiting resource. The first type of decision is
exemplified by the choice of which crop to plant on each plot;
the second type by the technical decisions of how intensively
to plant, how much and what type of fertilizer to use, and the
like.

Now the first type of decision is a choice among a finite
number of qualitatively different alternatives. There are, to
carry on our example, only a finite number of different crops
and, like horses and apples, they are incommensurable. The
second type of decision is infinitesimal and quantitative; it
is a question of how much is to be used of each input and how
much is to be produced of the outputs. Now the point of departure of the marginal analysis is the second type of decision whereas the point of departure of linear programming is
the first.

It is clearly possible to extend the marginal analysis so
that it deals with both types of decision. The method is simply
to introduce a variable for each qualitatively different kind of

input and output, and to introduce all these variables into the
production function. The function is then solved in the usual
way, except that no solution is considered admissable which requires negative outputs or inputs. This device is somewhat arti-
ficial, and may be complicated mathematically, but it does serve
the purpose of bringing the entire production problem onto the
conceptual framework of the marginal analysis. And it does, of
course, lead to the important theorems outlined in chapter i.

Linear programming can also be extended to deal with both
types of decision. The technique is the one suggested by Koopmans of treating each variation in technical proportions as a
separate process. Again the price is mathematical awkwardness,
and the gain is the treatment of the entire production problem
by means of a unified theory.

But clearly there is an advantage in recognizing the existence of two dissimilar problems here and in treating each of
them by the appropriate analytic procedure. There is an advantage, too, in perceiving that in different firms and contexts
one or the other of the problems may be of preëminent importance. With respect to industrial firms, for example, there is
frequently little scope for variation within the processes (see
Noyes, 28; pp. 61-62) while the important decisions concern
choices among a finite number of basically different technical
operations. Linear programming, therefore, appears to be
peculiarly adapted to the analysis of industrial programs.

3. *The Problem of Time*

We are not yet done with exploring the implications of assuming
that the number of technological alternatives in production is
finite. And we have yet an additional peculiarity of the linear
programming formulation to consider. This new peculiarity is the
shape of the supply curves considered.

In the usual mode of analysis, the supply curves for factors
of production are generally thought of as sloping gradually upward, to the right. Thus, limitations on economic activity
arise, typically, from the increasing expensiveness of supplies.
In linear programming, on the other hand, a different type of
limitation plays the central role. Inputs are thought of as

being available at constant unit cost up to a certain maximum, and thereafter not available at all. The supply curve is assumed to be a horizontal line up to the limiting quantity, and there to become infinitely inelastic. Linear programming thus deals with situations where the supplies of some, at least, of the inputs are limited absolutely at some finite level. This peculiarity arises because in linear programming attention is focused on limitations of productive opportunities which result from the finite capacity of the economic unit in question.

Both of these assumptions relate, though in different ways, to finiteness and both are consequences of dealing with a static model. We shall discuss first the assumption of an absolute limitation on the supply of resources.

From the point of view of an individual firm it is easy to see how such limitations come about. Hicks has described it as follows:

> The entrepreneur already has under his control
> a complex of goods, the equipment of the firm.
> Equipment includes land, buildings, machinery,
> tools, raw materials, goods in process, goods
> technically finished but not yet sold. Now it
> does seem reasonable to assume that this equip-
> ment will have acquired some organic unity, so
> that it cannot be exactly reduplicated at a
> moment's notice. It is the firm's legacy from
> the past, and, as such, does seem to constitute
> a block of 'fixed resources' in the relevant
> sense. (16; pp. 199-200.)

To Hicks' catalogue of fixed resources there should probably be added the permanent and integrated staff of the establishment. Within a short time-period these resources limit absolutely the opportunities available to the firm, and in a dynamic context they limit the firm's rate of growth.

In a dynamic model there is no fixed limit on the supply of re- sources available to a firm. In fact, the growth of a firm may be described by means of the increase in its capacity, that is, in its supply of durable resources. There is, however, an analagous restriction in the dynamic case. Clearly there is a limit to the rate at which any firm can create or absorb new resources; and this maximum rate of growth provides a limit to the activity of the firm in each successive time period. Dynamic models involving limited rates of expansion have been studied by von Neumann (39), and Wood (45). Such models require careful dating of all inputs and outputs and place limits on the inputs of each time period in terms of the outputs of preceding time periods. With these exceptions they are similar to the static models discussed in the present essay, and the methods of analysis are identical.

Absolute limitations on the supply of resources provide a plausible description of the economic problem of an entire nation or other closed economy. From a global point of view a certain quantity of each resource is available for use, and no more can be obtained for the present. To be sure, it may not be worth while to use some of the resources, such as infertile lands, low-grade ores, obsolete machinery, unskilled man power. But only a certain quantity of high-grade ore is available at any time and if more metal is wanted low-grade ores will have to be used. Similarly, the supply of fertile land is limited and agricultural output can be increased only by extending the margin of cultivation or by altering the processes for the use of fertile land in the direction of more intensive use.

It will be seen that the absolute limitation on the supply of each resource is a consequence of our insistence that the units of each resource be strictly homogeneous. Outputs may become more expensive as quantities increase if they require use of inferior resources or processes, but the supply curves for raw materials can never rise gradually. Those parts of the supply which would lie on a rising supply curve in conventional treatments are considered to be different inputs in this context. Here, as previously, we see that apparent novelties are less statements of new facts than they are new modes of expression. The justification for such new modes of expression is, of course, their usefulness in the description and analysis of familiar phenomena.

The assumption that the number of productive processes available is finite is also a time-limited assumption. It is true of any short-time period to the extent that the number of types of industrial equipment in existence for accomplishing any given objective is limited. It is true over considerable periods for many industries. For example, overland transportation can be accomplished by inland waterway, road, rail, or air. The choice of route between any two points is also limited. In this field, then, the number of processes from among which to select is finite and remains so for considerable periods.

The same illustration shows the conditions under which the range of choice may become infinite. This occurs whenever a new road or airfield or rail line is to be constructed. It occurs in an industrial context whenever a machine is to be designed for some purpose instead of being taken off the shelf. In the long run we are constantly redesigning and rebuilding our economic equipment, but in the short run we are as constantly adapting to present purposes the finite number of varieties of equipment inherited from the past.

It appears from this discussion that linear programming and the marginal analysis treat somewhat different problems. The marginal analysis deals with the long-run trend of choice in a static situation, that is, with the designs that would be adopted if the economic situation stood still long enough for the gradual modernization of equipment to catch up with it. Linear programming explores the short-run expedients of a dynamic situation, that is, the optimum utilization in the current juncture of the more or less inappropriate equipment currently available.

The nature of the compromises which linear programming finds to be necessary became most evident in chapter ii. In that chapter we found that it was frequently advisable to use several processes simultaneously merely because the facilities for these processes were available while the facilities needed for a single process, perfectly adapted to the current situation, were not. If, by good chance, there were to exist a single process which conformed to the current supply and demand situation, linear programming would lead to the use of that process alone. But, except in the very long run, such situations are likely to be exceptional.

4. *Variations of Linear Programming*

This book is principally concerned with a single type of linear programming: the analysis of a firm under static conditions where the production, supply, and demand functions are all assumed to be known. In assessing the place of this method in the economist's kit of tools, however, it is necessary to catalogue, at least in

summary fashion, the varying forms to which linear programming lends
itself.

Linear programming models vary in several dimensions, so to speak.
With regard to time they may be static (like the ones discussed in
this essay) or dynamic. With regard to entrepreneurial knowledge,
the relevant supply, demand, and production functions may be assumed to be known or else specified by conditional probability
distributions. With regard to scope they may deal with a single
firm, or even with a smaller unit, with an industry, or with an
entire economic system. With regard to logical structure the restraints imposed may leave room for optimization, as was done
throughout this essay, or the restraints may be sufficient to determine completely the economic activities contained in the model,
as in Leontief's studies and some recent work in the Department of
the Air Force.

Each of the variations opens the way to a possible field of
application, and each presents its peculiar mathematical and statistical problems. It seems worth while to say a few words about
dynamic models, so-called stochastic models, and general equilibrium models.

Economists are familiar with the way in which a dynamic mode
of analysis may be developed from a static one, and the usual procedure applies in linear programming. Static linear programming
rests on the relationships by which quantities of homogeneous goods
and services (inputs) are transformed into other homogeneous goods
and services (outputs), as we have seen. If we consider a production program as continuing over a number of periods of time,
specify the quantity of each input and output that becomes available at the beginning of each period as a function of activities
in earlier periods, and seek to determine the level of each process in each period, the framework of a dynamic analysis results.
A genuine dynamic quality is imparted to the analysis when the
limitations on the activities of any period are expressed in terms
of the results of previous periods. In this way a feedback is
introduced into the system, and the successive periods are linked
together by a set of linear difference equations which determine
the maximum rate of growth of the system, the level of operation
of each process during each period, and any inherent tendency to
cyclical behavior. A simple model of this type has been present-

ed by Wood (45). Such a system was used more than a decade ago by von Neumann (39) to determine the relationship between the physical growth of an economy and the rate of interest. More recently Hawkins (15) has used a closely related model to study cyclical instability.

Dynamic models are particularly adapted to the study of self-contained organizations whose current activities are to a significant extent dependent on their own recent past. They do not appear to be readily applicable to the study of individual firms or industries which can procure necessary equipment from outside and can finance such procurement by recourse to external sources of credit.

One of the most important fields for the future development of linear programming lies in the direction of stochastic models. By assuming that the relevant market and technological functions are known the sort of models considered in this essay evade the most critical problems which confront an entrepreneur. Knight and others have made familiar the notion that the heart of the entrepreneur's function is to shoulder the risks of economic enterprise and to assume the responsibility for reaching decisions in areas of ignorance. These risks result specifically from the fact that the relevant economic functions are not, and in the nature of the case cannot be, known. By assuming them known, linear programming has been enabled to reduce the entrepreneur's problem to the level of industrial engineering and to solve it in terms of engineering formulas. This solution is presented in all diffidence as an aid and guide to the entrepreneur and economist and without the intention of turning the entrepreneurial function over to electronic calculating machines. It is of assistance to the entrepreneur to have at hand the implications of any assumed set of economic functional relationships, but he is still faced by the need for evaluating the uncertainties of the case and weighing the likelihood that an assumed set of relationships will actually obtain.

There is little reason to hope that linear programming, or any other simple formulized technique, will be able to comprehend this entire problem. But it does appear probable that linear programming can take a useful step in this direction by working with conditional probability distributions instead of definite functional relationships. This line of work has not yet been implemented, although there is reason to hope that useful results can be obtained.

The study of stochastic models — that is, models which incorporate probability distributions — is needed also from a statistical point of view. One of the preëminent advantages of linear programming is that its analysis is carried out entirely in terms of measurable relationships so that it can be applied empirically. But such application requires the empirical determination of the constants of the relationships, and such determinations are subject to statistical error. At the present time there is no adequate theory for determining the effect of errors in the constants on the final results of the analysis, and a study of stochastic models is needed to throw light on this problem.

Stochastic models for linear programming are at present a conceptual possibility which may be expected to become an actuality within a few years. At present, none are available.

The scope of economic activity to be included in a linear programming model is obviously a matter of choice. The models considered in this study relate to a single enterprise, but the earliest empirical studies of linear programming covered the entire American economy (Cornfield, 4; Leontief, 23). Global descriptions of economic inter-relationships have been a traditional concern of economists since the time of Quesnay, at least, and Leontief, the pioneer of the field, has expressed his indebtedness to the *Tableau Economique* and the general equilibrium model of Walras. But, by contrast with earlier formulations, linear programming emphasises the physical inter-relationships of productive processes almost to the exclusion of the demand side. Leontief, indeed, has gone to the extent of eliminating all scope for choice from his model. He regards as technologically fixed the quantity of each input required per unit of output for every industry, and for his purposes households are an industry with labor services as an output and consumption goods as inputs. Once this framework has been adopted, the relative levels of activity of all industries and the relative prices of their outputs are determinate.

More recent work (cf. Koopmans, 19; Samuelson, 33) has added scope for flexibility to global models, but in such studies a single criterion for optimization and a centralized decision unit are assumed. In the Walrasian general equilibrium, of course, each consumer is regarded as an independent decision unit striving to maximize his own utility index. The Walrasian equilibrium system can be expressed readily in terms of the conceptual apparatus of linear programming. Indeed, both Walras (41) and his follower, Cassell (2) assumed that production functions were linear and homogeneous (a restriction later removed by Pareto (29)) so that the mathematical structure of their analysis is formally very close to that of linear programming. All these theories, however, make explicit use of the indifference maps of consumers and, therefore, are infeasible from the point of view of empirical implementation. The hope for the useful application of linear programming to problems of general equilibrium lies in following either of two leads: that of Leontief, who used established social and technical norms in lieu of economic choices, or that of Koopmans and Dantzig, who use rather simple social optima in place of unascertainable individual maximizing functions.

These considerations help define the scope for application of linear programming models of general equilibrium. If the lead of Leontief be followed, the method becomes useful for cataloguing, compiling, and cross-checking descriptive statistical data on industrial activity and, to some extent, for studying the internal self-consistency of possible constellations of economic activities. For example it can be used for studying the feasibility of a proposed housing program in the light of the capacity of the lumber and other supporting industries and of the needs of other industries which compete with housing for raw materials. If the lead of Koopmans be followed, the method can serve as a guide for the implementation of a well-formulated social objective. Economic mobilization for war production is an outstanding example of such a unified social objective. To the extent that a general social welfare function can be formulated, linear programming can be used to measure the extent to which various components of the economy are contributing to it. It is, of course, debatable whether centralized planning is the optimum method for achieving a centralized social objective (cf. Koopmans, 21; Lippincott, 25) but recent war experience has indicated that a certain amount of centralized control is necessary in practice whenever such an objective is considered paramount, and linear programming presents a systematic and promising method for attaining a balanced program by means of such controls.

In analyzing centralized planning by means of the Koopmans-Dantzig approach it is necessary to consider the diminishing usefulness of additional units of each type of output as the supplies become more plentiful. The methods given in chapter iii, above, apply in such analyses.

5. *What is Linear Programming*

In the course of this study we have considered one type of linear programming in great detail and have alluded to many other types. At the outset (chap. i, sec. 3) we attempted a definition of linear programming, but, lacking perspective, it had to be formalistic and perhaps uninformative. Now we are in a better position to set forth the distinguishing characteristics of this new technique.

Again and again in the course of our work we have invoked the notion of the *process*. All other aspects of the treatment, linearity, the possibility of optimization, limitations on the supply of resources, have been found to occur in some, but not all, variations of the method, but the central position of the process remained as a connecting thread throughout. The technique, indeed, might better be called "process analysis."

The process, it will be remembered, is simply one or more functional relationships in which all the inputs and outputs enter as dependent variables and there is only one independent variable, the "level" of the process. For all processes considered in this study the functional relationships were linear but, it was mentioned, this characteristic, though convenient in practice, is not essential in theory.

Entrepreneurial or social choice in this formulation consists in selecting the levels of a set of processes; such a set of levels is called a "program." There is room for substitution in this conceptual framework, but it is the substitution of processes rather than that of individual inputs or outputs. The core of any linear programming model is the set of process equations which specify the quantities of inputs and outputs as a function of the levels of the various processes.

In nearly all linear programming problems limitations exist on at least some of the inputs. These limitations typically take the form of inequalities; the total consumption of a limited input must not exceed some predetermined amount, though it may fall short of it. If the resulting program uses the total available supply of any input, that input has an implicit price which can be computed readily; otherwise that input is a free good.

Perhaps the most striking theoretical result of linear program-

ming was its explanation of the fact that several different processes are typically used simultaneously for producing similar
outputs or making use of a set of inputs. We explained this by
noting that the limitations on a productive program are histori-
cally determined and not, except by fortunate circumstance, in
precise accord with current demands. Thus it appeared that what
linear programming studies, in essence, is the process of adap-
tation of a slowly changing heritage of resources to a more
rapidly changing economic environment. Even where linear programming is static, it presumes a dynamic context. Dynamically
conceived, on the other hand, linear programming traces the
process whereby the stock of resources evolves in response to
the pressure of changing needs.

This, in outline, is the method and subject matter of linear
programming. In philosophy it is insistently practical. Its
concepts have been defined with an eye to statistical and engineering measurement, its problem is formulated so as to be a
simplified parallel to the problem of the entrepreneur or economic policy-maker. In the end, the method will stand or fall in
the measure of the value of its contribution to practical economic and industrial problems.

It is too early to tell what this contribution will be. In
the government already, Wood's group in the Department of the
Air Force and Evans' group in the Bureau of Labor Statistics have
produced results of considerable usefulness. Their work has been
hampered by paucity of statistics, by shortcomings in the theory,
some of which have been discussed above, and by the overwhelming
computational problems of dealing with large numbers of simultaneous relationships. Research designed to overcome all these difficulties is currently being prosecuted vigorously, and the outlook
is favorable. The study of the economic applications and implications of the method has lagged behind the other directions of
research, for the emphasis to date has been administrative rather
than economic. Now it appears that economists can rely on the
mathematicians, the electronicists, and the statisticians to provide a practical tool. What valid economic use is to be made of
this tool depends largely on the success of the economists in
adapting the concepts we have been discussing to their problems.

References

1. Boulding, Kenneth E. *Economic Analysis*. New York: Harper and Brothers, 1941.

2. Cassel, Gustav. *The Theory of Social Economy*. London: T. Fisher Unwin, Ltd., 1923, I, 134-142.

3. Chamberlin, E. H. *The Theory of Monopolistic Competition*. Cambridge: Harvard University Press, 1938.

4. Cornfield, Jerome, W. Duane Evans, and Marvin Hoffenberg. *Full Employment Patterns, 1950*. Washington: U. S. Department of Labor, Serial No. R. 1868, 1947.

5. Cournot, Augustin. *Researches into the Mathematical Principles of the Theory of Wealth*. New York: Macmillan Co., 1927.

6. Dantzig, George B. *A Procedure for Maximizing a Linear Function Subject to Linear Inequalities.** Washington: Headquarters, U. S. Air Force, Comptroller, 1948.

7. ——. *A Proof of the Equivalence of the Programming Problem and the Game Problem.** Washington: Headquarters, U. S. Air Force, Comptroller, 1950.

8. ——. *Maximization of a Linear Form whose Variables are Subject to a System of Linear Inequalities.** Washington: Headquarters, U. S. Air Force, Comptroller, 1949.

9. ——. "Programming of Interdependent Activities, II, Mathematical Model." *Econometrica*, XVII (1949), 200-211.

10. Dean, Joel. *The Relation of Cost to Output for a Leather Belt Shop*. New York: National Bureau of Economic Research, 1941.

11. Eiteman, Wilford J. *Price Determination: Business Practice versus Economic Theory*. Ann Arbor: University of Michigan, School of Business Administration, 1949.

* Asterisks (*) denote references which have been circulated in mimeographed, dittoed, or similar form.

12. Gale, David, H. W. Kuhn, and A. W. Tucker. *Four Equivalent Linear-Convex Problems.** Princeton: 1949.

13. Gordon, R. A. " Short Period Price Determination," *American Economic Review,* XXXVIII (1948), 265-288.

14. Hall, R. L. and C. J. Hitch. " Price Theory and Business Behavior," *Oxford Economic Papers,* II (May, 1939), 12-45.

15. Hawkins, David. " Some Conditions of Macroeconomic Stability," *Econometrica,* XVI (1948), 309-322.

16. Hicks, J. R. *Value and Capital.* Oxford: Oxford University Press, 1941.

17. Jevons, William Stanley. *Political Economy.* London: Macmillan Co., 1878.

18. Knight, Frank H. *Risk, Uncertainty and Profit.* Boston and New York: Houghton Mifflin Co., 1921.

19. Koopmans, Tjalling C. *A Mathematical Model of Production.** Cowles Commission Discussion Paper: Economics: No. 262. Chicago: Cowles Commission for Research in Economics, 1949.

20. Koopmans, T. C. and S. Reiter. *Allocation of Resources in Production.** Cowles Commission Discussion Paper: Economics: No. 264. Chicago: Cowles Commission for Research in Economics, 1949.

21. Koopmans, T. C. *Efficient Allocation of Resources** Cowles Commission Discussion Paper: Economics 271B. Chicago: Cowles Commission for Research in Economics, 1949.

22. ——. *Systems of Linear Production Function** Santa Monica: Rand Corporation, 1948.

23. Leontief, Wassily W. *The Structure of American Economy. 1919-1929: An Empirical Application of Equilibrium Analysis.* Cambridge: Harvard University Press, 1941.

24. Lester, Richard A. " Shortcomings of Marginal Analysis for Wage-Employment Problems." *American Economic Review,* XXXVI (1946), 63-82.

25. Lippincott, Benjamin E., ed. *On the Economic Theory of Socialism*. Minneapolis: University of Minnesota Press, 1938.

26. Marshall, Alfred. *Principles of Economics*. 8th ed.; London: Macmillan Co., 1946.

27. Menger, Carl. *Grundsätze der Volkswirthschaftslehre*. London: London School of Economics, 1934.

28. Noyes, C. Reinold. "Memorandum on Costs in Relation to Output," in Joel Dean. *The Relation of Cost to Output for a Leather Belt Shop,* New York: National Bureau of Economic Research, 1941.

29. Pareto, Vilfredo. *Manuel d'économie politique*. Paris: V Giard et E. Briere, 1909, p. 605 ff.

30. Ricardo, David. *The Principles of Political Economy and Taxation*. London and Toronto: J. M. Dent & Sons, 1933.

31. Robinson, Joan. *The Economics of Imperfect Competition*. London: Macmillan Co., 1946.

32. Samuelson, Paul Anthony. *Foundations of Economic Analysis*. Cambridge: Harvard University Press, 1948.

33. ———. *Market Mechanisms and Maximization.** Santa Monica: Rand Corporation, 1949.

34. Say, Jean-Baptiste. *Economie Politique*. Paris: Guillaumin et Cie., 1888.

35. Senior, Nassau William. *Political Economy*. London: Charles Griffin and Co., 1872.

36. U. S. Air Force, Project SCOOP. *Scientific Planning of Military Programs, No. 4-PU.** Washington: Headquarters, U. S. Air Force, 1948.

37. ———. *Scientific Planning Techniques, No. 1-DU** Washington: Headquarters, U. S. Air Force, 1948.

38. Viner, Jacob. "Cost Curves and Supply Curves," *Zeitschrift für Nationalökonomie,* III (1931) 23-46.

39. Von Neumann, J. "A Model of General Equilibrium," *Review of Economic Studies*, XIII (1945-1946), 1-9.

40. Von Neuman, John, and Oskar Morgenstern. *Theory of Games and Economic Behavior*. Princeton: Princeton University Press, 1944.

41. Walras, Leon. *Elements d'économie politique pure ou théorie de la richesse sociale*. 2d ed.; Lausanne: F. Rouge, 1889, 20e Lecon, "Equations de la production."

42. Weyl, H. "The Elementary Theory of Convex Polyhedra", in *Contributions to the Theory of Games*, ed. H. W. Kuhn and A. W. Tucker. Princeton: Princeton University Press, 1950. Pp 3-18.

43. Wood, Marshall K. and Murray A. Geisler. *Development of Dynamic Models for Program Planning.* * Washington: Headquarters, U. S. Air Force, Comptroller, 1949.

44. Wood, Marshall K. and George B. Dantzig. "Programming of Interdependent Activities, I, General Dicsussion," *Econometrica*, XVII (1949), 193-199.

45. Wood, Marshall K. "Scientific Techniques for Program Planning," *Air University Quarterly Review*, III (1949), 49-65.

46. Kuhn, H. W. and A. W. Tucker. "Non-Linear Programming," in *Second Berkeley Symposium on Mathematical Statistics and Probability*, ed. Jerzy Neyman. Berkeley: University of California Press, in press.

www.ingramcontent.com/pod-product-compliance
Lightning Source LLC
Chambersburg PA
CBHW021944220326
41599CB00013BA/1671

* 9 780520 339439 *